SHELBY MUSTANG

RANDY LEFFINGWELL & DAVID NEWHARDT

MOTORBOOKS

To the late Bob Negstad and the late Tony Souza. We miss them both.

ACKNOWLEDGMENTS

OUR THANKS GO, FIRST AND FOREMOST, TO CARROLL SHELBY. He gave his time generously to this project, encouraging it from the start and patiently answering questions. In addition, he generously opened his shops to let us shoot some of the cars from his own collection.

For his help with those cars, for his sense of humor, for additional information and insight into Shelby Mustangs, and for his willingness to let us shoot very early and very late one long day and to wait patiently for trains, we thank Gary Patterson, general manager at Shelby Automobiles, Las Vegas.

In addition, we wish to thank Peter Brock for his time, for long conversations, for the hospitality he and Gayle so generously offered, and for his own contributions to making this history. We also are grateful to Dave Friedman for his amazing stories.

In addition, we must express our gratitude to retired Ford stylists Gale Halderman and Joe Oros, who provided plentiful background on the design process that produced the notchback and created the fastback Mustangs, and on the brief rise and fall of a Shelby Mustang body; to retired Ford chief engineer Howard Freers, who elaborated on the engineering decisions made for the introductory model;

and to retired product planner John Onken, who explained in detail how cars came into being at Ford Motor Company during the 1960s.

Further, we are deeply grateful to Anne Roeske and to Jerry Malewski for their memories of a fascinating and fateful day at the Waterford Hills Road Racing circuit.

Our deep gratitude goes to retired racer Jim Gessner for sharing the wonderful stories of campaigning Hertz's Rent-A-Racer in the Washington, D.C., area.

Our sincere thanks also go to Hau Thai-Tang, Ford's director for advanced product planning, Special Vehicle Team (SVT), who patiently answered hundreds of questions at the New York Auto Show.

The late Bob Negstad, Ford senior engineer, spent hours talking with each of us separately about Mustangs, Cobras, and GT40s. Each of us misses having dinner with you at the café on Telegraph, Bob.

Numerous journalists and authors have written about and documented the story of Shelby's Mustangs. We must acknowledge and express our appreciation, in particular, to: Peter Brock; Dave Friedman; Richard Kopec, as editor along with Greg Kolasa, Vincent Liska, David Mathews, Carol Padden, Howard Pardee, Curt Vogt, and Douglas Waschenko; Trevor Legate; Leo Levine; Richard

Nisley; and Wallace Wyss. Without the work of these individuals over the past three decades, this book would have been much more difficult and the story much more challenging to sort out.

Shelby owners willingly opened their garages, at all hours, to get the right light. Thanks to all of you; this book wouldn't have been possible without your help. In no particular order: Len and Linda Perham; Stephen Nemeth; Doug Blake; Christian Briggs; Bill Hammerstein; Bill and Deb Warren; Gary Spraggins; Charley Lillard; Doug Bohrer; Michael Stewart; Willie Ashford; Don Chambers; James "JimBo" and Julie Black; Rob Walton; Gordon Gimbel; Jonathan Peck; and Larry Freeman.

Our deepest thanks to Craig Jackson and Steve Davis of the Barrett-Jackson Auction Company for letting us play with their toys.

We extend special gratitude to Bruce Meyer, whose encouragement and assistance has often made the impossible look easy.

Drew Alcazar is one of this hobby's consummate car guys. For this book he is one of our heroes, finding for us some of the rarest of rare cars. We are sincerely grateful.

Many individuals helped us arrange cars to shoot, opened doors, and answered endless questions: Alan Hall and John Clor of SVT; Arturo Quiroga; John Clinard; Harold Allen; Sandra Badgett; Jason Camp; and Jayna Dougherty of Ford Public Affairs; Dan Erickson, Ford Motor Company Still Images Library; and Jim Muise, Scott Black, and the crew at Unique Performance.

A tip of the hat, and many thanks, to the management of the Las Vegas Motor Speedway, for our wonderful time spent on their drag strip.

This book came into being as the late Tony Sousa was reviewing the color proofs of *Mustang: Forty Years* and he asked when Shelbys were going to get a book like that. Here it is, Tony; we miss you.

Last, but never least, we thank our spouses, Carolyn Chandler Leffingwell and Susan Newhardt, for their continuing encouragement and patience.

—Randy Leffingwell
Santa Barbara, California

—David Newhardt
Pasadena, California

First published in 2007 by Motorbooks, an imprint of MBI Publishing Company, Galtier Plaza, Suite 200, 380 Jackson Street, St. Paul, MN 55101-4810 USA

Motorbooks titles are also available at discounts in bulk quantity for industrial or sales-promotional use. For details write to Special Sales Manager at MBI Publishing Company, Galtier Plaza, Suite 200, 380 Jackson Street, St. Paul, MN 55101-4810 USA.

To find out more about Shelby Mustang, join us online at www.motorbooks.com.

ISBN-13: 978-0-7603-3202-3
ISBN-10: 0-7603-3202-9

Printed in China

On the cover: Functional scoops in front of the rear wheels directed cooling air to the rear brakes. Lessons learned on the track were applied to the road cars.

On the frontispiece: Carroll Shelby poses with his 1969 lineup. The roll bar was less substantial than the 1968 model. Only the center NACA fed air to the air cleaner; the remaining four handled engine compartment cooling duties.

On the title page: Ah, the good life. With a curb weight of 3,850 pounds, road imperfections were beat into submission. Ford insisted the Shelby road cars adopt an increasingly mainstream approach, but they eventually started to compete with the high-performance Mustangs.

On the back cover: With 450-plus horsepower, the 2007 GT500 is a tire dealer's dream come true. Its SVT development ensures that it will be durable and fast—very fast.

CONTENTS

INTRODUCTION

BY AUGUST 1964, FORD MOTOR COMPANY MANAGE-MENT KNEW THAT BOTH GENERAL MOTORS AND CHRYSLER WERE TAKING THE MUSTANG SERIOUSLY. Dealers were selling the car, conceived as "a car for the ladies but which the men would enjoy driving," faster than anyone had guessed.

Rumors drifted over to Dearborn from GM's Technical Center in Warren that Chevrolet had a challenger to the Mustang that it would release for 1967. Plymouth had already beaten Ford to the market when its Valiant-based Barracuda reached dealers on April 1, two weeks ahead of the new Mustang. Though the Barracuda arrived first, Chrysler Corporation had introduced the car at a $2,365 six-cylinder base price, about $45 more than Ford had set for a comparable Mustang.

Ford had successfully capitalized on the excitement that began in October 1962 when engineers introduced their two-seat mid-engine prototype called the Mustang. The production car kept only the name, and Ford's experience with its two-seat Thunderbird taught them that four seats sold better. But Lee Iacocca's philosophy was that any exciting vehicle was fine if it set up the youth market to wait until the company introduced the four-seater 18 months later.

Without the energy that this anticipation created, Chrysler barely kept up. Through 1964 and 1965, Plymouth sold barely 85,000 units even after Chrysler engineer Scott Harvey created the Formula S package for 1965 that provided a 235-horsepower 273-cid V-8 and a more sporting suspension. However, Ford product planners knew that while Plymouth planned a mild update for the car in 1966, for 1967 Chrysler was re-skinning the automo-bile and designer Milt Antonick's new lines would trans-form the car away from the fastback Valiant it had been.

Chevrolet's Corvette offered the most substantial threat to the Mustang. GM's two-seater offered a 360-horsepower fuel-injected engine in 1963 and Chevy would have 375-horsepower for 1964. GM stylists Peter Brock and Chuck Pohlmann had originated and developed the 1963 Stingray's design. The striking body which Larry Shinoda made ready for production had raised an understandable commotion not only in the U.S. but in Europe as well. Ford management easily could imagine that the second- and third-year updates and facelifts would further enhance the car's appearance.

Pontiac Division posed a new threat as well with an option for its compact Tempest in 1964 named the G.T.O. after an exotic racing Ferrari. Pontiac would offer a "tri-power" 389-cid V-8 producing 348 horsepower. In an era of 30-cent gasoline, these were the first shots fired in the performance war. Mustang assembly plants worked overtime to satisfy the demand. But no one in Ford's World Headquarters expected this to last for ever.

The broad reach of Ford's "Total Performance" program recently had taken Mustangs to Europe to com-pete in the combined road race and track contest known as the Tour de France and another through the Alps called the Monte Carlo Rally. Prior to that, in January 1962, it had shipped Ford engines to England to help create the Shelby A.C. Cobra.

Texas farmer and successful car racer Carroll Shelby had conceived this hybrid sports car after a similar idea of his had failed using Corvette engines in exotic car bodies from Italy's Scalietti. These simple Ford-powered, two-seat, English sports cars had led struggling A.C. Cars away from the brink of extinction and to a healthy comeback. At the same time, Cobras captured the hearts and minds of journalists and performance car fans as they seized nearly every checkered flag they went after.

In late 1963, attempting to overcome the aerodynamic drag limitations of the blocky open cars, Peter Brock, who had left Chevrolet Styling and joined Shelby, designed the beautiful and devastatingly effective Shelby Cobra Daytona coupe. At that point as Shelby's operations were growing, he needed more space. He found a facility available in Venice, California, north of Los Angeles International Airport (LAX). Here Shelby and his staff produced racing and street Cobras. Throughout 1964 Shelby American Ford-powered Cobras continued taking on Ferraris, racing Corvettes, and all other comers.

By summer, a consensus had gained momentum among Ford division personnel. It was time to bring Shelby's imagination, skill, and racing prowess back home to the United States. Several engineers within Ford Division wanted to take the Mustang racing, and other competitors outside the company already had inquired about parts that might improve handling, braking, and performance.

In a meeting with Lee Iacocca, Shelby learned that Ford's Ray Geddes had gotten nowhere trying to get the Mustang recognized as a "production race car" for Sports Car Club of America (SCCA) competition in the United States. Shelby first had met Geddes, who held a masters degree in business and a law degree, when Ford's product planning chief Don Frey had brought him in to help Shelby manage the business end of the Cobra project in mid-1962.

As Peter Brock recalled, Shelby initially resisted getting involved with production Mustangs. He had Cobra roadsters racing throughout the world. For months by this time his new six-car Daytona Cobra Coupe program vigilantly battled against Henry Ford II's arch racing enemy Enzo Ferrari for the world manufacturers' championship. This was in addition to launching Ford's other program with Holman-Moody to campaign the new GT40s against Ferrari as well. However, from his days racing in the United States, Shelby knew John Bishop, the executive director of the SCCA. Ford Motor Company already had done Shelby some favors. After some delay, the Texan agreed to get involved. He told Iacocca he believed he knew what it would take to run the Mustang in Bishop's events.

Bishop told Shelby that to qualify for production classes, the car had to be a two-seater and that either the suspension or the engine could be modified for racing, but not both. The major hurdle was that Shelby had to manufacture 100 cars by January 1, 1965, to be eligible to race that year. Bishop hinted that he thought this was impossible to accomplish in less than five months. But John Bishop didn't understand the potential of a large corporation when competition motivated the principal decision makers. Within another five years, John Bishop, Enzo Ferrari, General Motors, Chrysler, and the rest of the automotive and racing world would grasp what was possible when Ford Motor Company committed its resources.

CHAPTER ONE

TOTAL PERFORMANCE POWERED BY FORD:
1960-1964, The Early Days

At the 1954 24 Hours of Le Mans race, Carroll Shelby and Paul Frère drove a non-supercharged 182-horsepower 1954 Aston Martin, similar to this 225-brake-horsepower supercharged DB3S-C.

Shelby and Frère retired in the eleventh hour of the 1954 Le Mans race while driving a 1954 Aston Martin DB3S. Introduced in 1953, Aston Martin built four that year, and another pair in 1954.

Carroll Shelby and Roy Salvadori drove this Aston Martin DBR1 to win Le Mans in 1959. The DBR1 first appeared in 1956 using Aston's 2.993-liter inline six, which by 1959 developed about 280 brake horsepower. The winners drove 4,348 kilometers (2,717.5 miles) averaging 181.2 kilometers per hour (113.3 miles per hour).

IN THE MID-1990s, A BEST-SELLING BOOK ADVANCED THE THEORY THAT THERE ARE NO COINCIDENCES, THERE ARE ONLY OPPORTUNITIES. James Redfield's novel, *The Celestine Prophecy*, told the tale of an adventurer off to Peru to find purpose and insight. Redfield could just as easily have stayed home and written a factual history of Carroll Shelby and the Ford-powered automobiles that bear his name. The lessons of either effort would have been similar: Stay alert. Be clever, creative, and charming. Get to the right place at the right time. And never lose sight of your goal, even when setbacks seem to steer you away. In Redfield's book, and Shelby's professional career, course alterations just provided even better opportunities.

Carroll Shelby found racing later in life than some of his contemporaries. At age 29 in May, 1952, he stuffed himself into a friend's box-stock MG T.C. and proceeded to win his first two races in his first two days of competition. To the car owner and others watching him, it seemed as though Shelby had the potential for greatness behind the wheel. His innate driving skill, ability to conserve the car, insight into handling and road holding, and a smattering of

good luck propelled him through a mostly successful first season. Arriving just before the start of a race in 1953, Shelby, whose day job was chicken farming, had no time to suit up. Unflustered, he won the event in an Anglo-American hybrid, an Allard powered by a Cadillac V-8. He liked its power and had learned to tame its unpredictable handling. When he stepped out of the car still dressed in his bib overalls to take the trophy, he instantly established this trademark. Not long after that he added a dark cowboy hat that remained part of his uniform for decades. In spring of 1954, he drove in Buenos Aires, where he met Aston Martin's team manager John Wyer. By June of that year, Wyer had Shelby sharing an Aston Martin DB3S with Paul Frère at Le Mans. Unfortunately, they retired from that race with a broken front stub axle.

Wyer offered Shelby more opportunities in 1955, starting with Sebring in one of Aston's team DBR sports racers. While that car broke before the race ended, Wyer was still impressed enough with Shelby to bring him along to Aintree, England, where the Texan finished second in a heavy rainstorm. For the rest of the year, Shelby floated

At the 1989 Monterey Historic Automobile Races, Aston Martin celebrated the 30th anniversary of its Le Mans win with a replica of the race pits, including the actual race cars campaigned. The center car, No. 5, won the race.

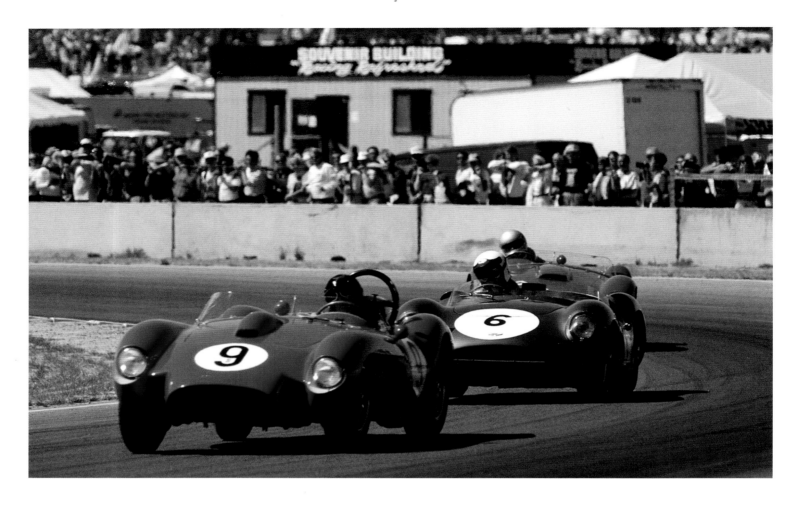

Ferrari entered 11 team and private cars in Le Mans in 1959, including five of its new 250 Testarossa models. Ferraris used 12-cylinder engines with 2,953-cc displacement. None of the Testarossas finished the 24-hour race, while Aston Martin finished number one and number two.

from Aston Martins in Europe, to Ferraris for Californian Tony Parravano in races on the West Coast, to Porsche Spyders for Porsche's racing director Huschke von Hanstein at other venues on the continent.

Shelby became an important sports car dealer in Dallas early in 1956, selling everything from Rolls-Royces to Elvas. This gave him the opportunity to stay around cars full time and away from chickens all the time. He raced Ferraris out west for another Californian, John Edgar, and back east for Ferrari's U.S. importer Luigi Chinetti in New York. By year end, both Tony Parravano and John Edgar

had fallen out of love with carmaker Enzo Ferrari, and both team owners had switched to Italy's other racing marque, Maserati. Throughout this time, Shelby not only drove, but also dreamed about and conceived his own idea for a racer. This would be a car in which he could compete as well as one he could sell to others. While he had raced and won in some of Europe's most exotic cars—12-cylinder Ferraris, 8-cylinder Maseratis, and 6-cylinder Astons—he knew that each of these marques was expensive to buy and costly to maintain. He eventually acquired the Cad-Allard he had raced back in Texas. While he left it at home, and while it

Left: **Carroll Shelby relaxes in the cockpit of a 1960 Maserati Tipo 61, similar to the race cars he drove that year with Masten Gregory in the Sebring 12-hour race.**

Below: **Ford kicked off its "Total Performance" campaign in January 1963 with the introduction of the Falcon Sprint 260-ci V-8 at the 1963 Monte Carlo Rally. This Falcon entered in the historic race was driven by Bosse Ljungfeldt, while Gunnar Haggbom acted as navigator. A broken clutch resulted in a 43rd place finish, despite noteworthy results on some of the later stages.** *David Friedman collection*

was unsophisticated, he knew he could repair it with parts available at service counters in any small town in North America. He considered other English-American hybrids and was the first to install Chevrolet engines into the Lister sports racers.

It galled Shelby that in European Grand Touring racing one manufacturer was ahead of a legion of others' makes and always seemed to win. What irked the Texan more was noticing that if Enzo Ferrari's cars didn't win, Il Commendatore (as those who worked for Enzo called him) either withdrew from the race series or found ways to influence rule makers to reclassify serious competitors—or outlaw them.

Back home, Shelby had watched Chevrolet's Corvettes run in national and international meets. But Chevrolet had

no factory racing effort, despite the vigorous efforts of engineer Zora Arkus-Duntov and tacit support from his boss, Ed Cole. Street racing and the large number of deadly crashes at organized races throughout the world in 1955 and 1956 had raised the eyebrows of a public audience growing increasingly safety conscious. Chevrolet and the other U.S. car manufacturers had co-signed an agreement in June 1957. The major U.S. automakers, as members of the Automobile Manufacturers Association (AMA), agreed that they would no longer support "speed events." So Chevrolet (along with Chrysler) offered only unofficial assistance that lacked the concentrated effort of factory engineering. And without that factory expertise, Corvettes never won international races.

It was obvious to Shelby that Ferrari was vulnerable.

Dave MacDonald (98) and teammate Bob Holbert debuted the Shelby King Cobras at Kent, Washington, in September 1963. Although both cars set records that day, and lead most of the race, they retired due to various minor mechanical problems. MacDonald would go onto win the next two races at Riverside and Laguna Seca and set records in doing it. Here MacDonald leads Jerry Grant's (8) Lotus 19-Buick and Rodger Ward's (1) Copper-Chevrolet at Kent. Note that the MacDonald car has yet to be painted in the Shelby team colors of Viking Blue. None of the original King Cobras are known to exist in spite of some very bad replicas that show up at various vintage events claiming to be original.

David Friedman collection

Carroll accepted the idea that beating the Italian team would take a concentrated effort with vast resources and support. Even as he concluded this, his chances for 1959 looked good. He had sold his Dallas dealership the previous year, which left him available to race in Europe again. Aston Martin had committed three new cars—their DBR1/300s—to Le Mans, and team manager John Wyer was determined to beat not only the Ferrari factory and private-entry 250GTs but also the few Jaguar D-Types he knew were entered.

Wyer was a meticulous planner. He calculated the speeds his cars needed to average around the track and around the clock in order to win an event. He relied on the other teams to be neither as prepared nor as durable, figuring they would break mechanical parts or crash. Things went according to plan and at 4 p.m. on Sunday, June 21, Shelby and English co-driver Roy Salvadori crossed the finish line first. They had accomplished 4,348

kilometers (2,717 miles) averaging 181.2 kilometers per hour (113.2 miles per hour). It was Aston Martin's tenth attempt, Salvadori's seventh try, and Shelby's second time entering the race (after 1954, also with Aston in the DB3S). Shelby and Salvadori finished 10 kilometers ahead of Aston teammates Maurice Trintignant and Paul Frère. But Carroll and Roy had run 346 kilometers (216 miles) beyond the nearest Ferrari, which finished in third place.

While prize money is awarded for winning Le Mans, or any race for that matter, something more accrues to those who go the distance in France: Name recognition.

Take a Cooper Monaco chassis, stuff in a 289-cubic-inch Ford V-8, and the result is the potent King Cobra. Only eight were built, but they were driven by the cream of the crop, including Dan Gurney, Parnelli Jones, and Dave MacDonald.

Shelby raced a Cad-Allard similar to this 1953 J2X in November 1952 at a road-racing course close to Caddo Mills, Texas. Early in his racing career, Shelby became familiar with hybrid vehicles, which are built by mounting one manufacturer's engine in another manufacturer's chassis.

A King Cobra, with Dave MacDonald behind the wheel, won the *Los Angeles Times* Grand Prix at Riverside and the Monterey Pacific Grand Prix at Laguna Seca, both in October 1963.

Throughout Europe, Carroll Shelby's name opened doors. In the United States, Shelby even appeared in a short run of Gillette razor advertisements. His win at Le Mans, however, added the needed impetus for a project that he had just initiated with Chevrolet's Ed Cole, fellow racer Jim Hall, a Fort Worth petroleum entrepreneur and Chevrolet dealer named Gary B. Laughlin, and a physician friend in Houston.

For relaxation and excitement, Laughlin raced his own

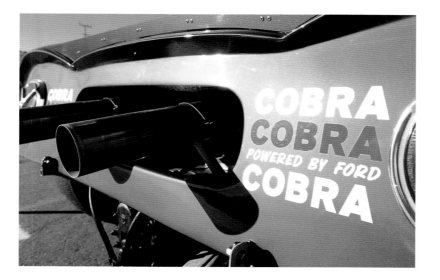

Ferrari 750 Monza in SCCA events, where he often encountered Hall and Shelby. Laughlin had grown tired of the huge Ferrari repair bills. Knowing it would be less expensive than most other production GTs, Carroll wanted to build a true GT version of the Corvette. This would be lighter in weight, probably enclosed as a coupe with a stylish Italian body. Shelby already knew Cole and Cole liked the idea of showing GM's flamboyant styling chief Bill Mitchell what a European design house could do with the Corvette. Shelby asked for and got three chassis as a pilot program. His initial goal was to produce enough of them to qualify for SCCA's B-production class, for him, Hall and Laughlin to race the cars themselves, and have other cars to sell to competitors. Shelby and Hall knew SCCA officials nationwide by this time. The two Texans understood what

Most competitors tended to get this view of the King Cobra, because its 289-cubic-inch engine, teamed with a lightweight Cooper Monaco chassis, allowed it to run away from most of the field.

Aerodynamics in sports car racing was in its infancy when the 1963 King Cobra hit the track. The large, open cockpit allowed for easy ingress and exit but didn't help airflow management. *Randy Leffingwell*

Early King Cobras suffered from overheating problems, but the fix was quick in coming. A front-mounted radiator helped balance the rear mid-engine configuration. *Randy Leffingwell*

The low-cut windshield did little to protect the driver, but helmets and goggles kept the bugs out of the driver's face. Here a King Cobra sweeps through Laguna Seca's famous "Corkscrew" turn at the Monterey Historic Automobile Races.

Early King Cobras used drag-style exhaust pipes, pointing straight up, but later vehicles utilized an equal-length exhaust system that exited through the rear panel.

it would take to build a legal race car and make it a winner.

In early 1960, as letters flew between Fort Worth, Texas, and Warren, Michigan, Shelby relocated to Southern California. He had raced there often enough to understand the existing hot-rod scene and to have witnessed the growing drag-racing community, which had fostered a large industry in high-performance equipment. Dean Moon was a king among those aftermarket parts makers and vendors. His shop in Santa Fe Springs, east of Los Angeles, was mecca for racers of all ages and abilities. Shelby rented an office in Moon's shops for $200 a month. Goodyear Tire & Rubber had awarded Carroll its racing tire distributorship for 11 western states, and he now had a business of his own to help support his goals.

Shelby succeeded in getting three complete Corvette chassis from Cole. He ordered two of these with four-speed manual gearboxes while the third had an automatic for Hall, who had faith that these transmissions would work for racing. Hall was convinced this would shorten lap times because drivers would lose no power while shifting gears. Shelby was in Italy regularly, and from his Ferrari trips he already had met Sergio Scaglietti, Ferrari's car-body fabricator. Shelby persuaded Scaglietti to modify fastback aluminum coupes based on Ferrari's 250 GT Tour de France bodies and shipped the three Corvette chassis to Modena. The job wasn't easy or quick. Scaglietti wanted $3,000 for

each finished car body but Shelby bargained him down to $2,500. The Corvette's wheel track stretched 4 inches wider than the Ferrari's. Scaglietti's panel beaters spent extra time adding aluminum panels to widen his bodies. But when they completed the cars with their spare, simple interiors, each Corvette coupe weighed in at 400 pounds less than Chevrolet's own open fiberglass-bodied cars.

While work continued on the cars, Cole contacted Shelby to tell him these three cars would be the only ones he would get. Zora Duntov and several others had gotten to the board of directors. Concerned that a lightweight Corvette coupe might beat their own roadsters, the board ordered Cole to end the project. For Shelby, the deal was over at that moment. Without chassis or at least engines in a pipeline, his dreams for a hundred of these cars evaporated.

Shelby still had hopes for his idea, however. Every experience taught the wise Texan crucial new lessons. Now he was ready, and he also had some conditions under which *he* preferred to operate. He not only wanted engines, but he also expected to get them at a wholesale price. More than that, he needed ready access to the engineers who designed and developed those engines. If he was racing, he couldn't afford to waste time playing politics from one weekend to the next.

The three-year period from 1959 through 1961 was pivotal for Shelby. Thinking he had pulled a muscle in his

With the driver set as far back as allowable, the 289-cubic-inch Cobra minimized the front/rear weight imbalance. Side-mounted exhaust pipes encouraged the use of driver ear plugs. *Randy Leffingwell*

chest early in 1959, he underwent a series of treatments that did no good. A year later, he sought a second opinion and his doctor diagnosed the symptoms as angina pectoris, in which an insufficient supply of blood to the heart causes severe convulsive pain. The doctor's verdict ended Shelby's racing career as a driver.

Six thousand miles away, in late summer of 1961 in the village of Thames Ditton in Surrey, England, Charles Hurlock and his brother William received chest-convulsing news themselves. Hurlock owned A.C. Cars Limited, a sports car producer with a modest output of adequately powered and fairly priced two-seat roadsters and four-seat fastbacks, some of which used engines from outside producers. Bristol Cars Ltd., a firm in the city of the same name, produced fast, stylish, and expensive touring cars. Its directors had chosen to stop manufacturing the 2-liter inline 6-cylinder engine that had, up to that point, powered his two-seat Ace—this 125-horse engine was good enough to push his Ace from 0 to 60 miles per hour in 8 seconds.

Ken Rudd, a Ford dealer in Worthing, England, and longtime A.C. enthusiast, provided Hurlock with Ford's 2.6-liter 125-horsepower inline six-cylinder engine from its top line Zephyr/Zodiac sedans. Properly configured, however, this engine served up 170 horsepower for racers and launched the Ace from 0 to 100 miles per hour in 8 seconds. The engine's smaller dimensions even allowed A.C. to lower the front hood and lengthen the nose behind a smaller grille, but this package never caught on. Hurlock scrambled for new alternatives, considering the six-cylinder XK engine from Jaguar, a V-8 from the Daimler SP250 two-seater, and even the new lightweight V-8 model from American Buick sedans. Unfortunately, the Jaguar six required extensive chassis redesign to mount in the A.C., Daimler never could reach agreeable terms with Hurlock, and Rover had secured U.K. rights for the Buick engine from General Motors. Shelby stayed current with all these developments through Ray Brock, his editor friend at *Hot Rod* magazine.

Cobras were intended to compete, and that means less is more. Going without bumpers was just one way to hold down weight in pursuit of more speed. *Randy Leffingwell*

A 289-cubic-inch competition Cobra races through Turn 8A at Laguna Seca Raceway at the 2003 Monterey Historic Automobile Races. Its short wheelbase demanded that its driver be particularly aware of weight transfer.

Randy Leffingwell

In the mid-1960s, most non-Cobra drivers saw this sight a lot. Significant power teamed with light weight and good reliability resulted in Cobra's taking the checkered flag more often than its competition.

Simple white-on-black instrumentation allows a driver to monitor engine conditions at a glance, which is crucial in a race. The lack of exterior door handles requires reaching inside for the latch. *Randy Leffingwell*

throughout Ford, a concept known as Total Performance: Powered by Ford.

In November 1960, Henry Ford II named Lee Iacocca vice president and general manager of Ford Division. At age 36 (a year younger than Carroll Shelby), Iacocca found himself in a position to redefine what Ford's blue oval logo meant to its customers and to young people. His predecessor Robert McNamara had brought out basic transportation in the form of the functional Falcon. Iacocca had given the company several bright marketing ideas and he understood that Ford, the man, now wanted more of this from Ford, the division.

Iacocca began meeting after hours with a think tank of eight sharp managers. They were Don Frey, head of product planning; Hal Sperlich, Frey's assistant for special projects; Bob Eggert, market research manager; Walter Murphy, Ford's public relations manager; marketing

A brace of Weber carburetors atop a 289-cubic-inch V-8 ensured plenty of fuel flowing at race speeds. Dual breathers on the valve covers vented crankcase pressure to the atmosphere. *Randy Leffingwell*

Three months before that, over the July 4 weekend, Shelby had been working the Pikes Peak Hill Climb in his role as Goodyear's racing tire distributor. While he was there, Brock introduced him to Dave Evans who was Ford Motor Company's representative for its competition engines. While the men talked racing, Evans confirmed some other information from Brock. First was that Ford had developed and perfected thin-wall casting techniques for engine blocks and within months it would announce a new 221-cubic-inch V-8 for the Fairlane model. Second was the philosophy that was spreading like wildfire

Only 16 USRRC Cobras were built in 1964; they were intended to compete in the United States Road Racing Championship series. This particular car raced four times, winning every time.

manager Chase Morsey; advertising manager John Bowers; and Sid Olson, from J. Walter Thompson, Ford's outside advertising agency. Ford's special projects manager Jacque Passino—essentially the company's racing manager even during the 1957 AMA ban—completed the group that quickly adopted the name "Fairlane Committee" because their dinner meetings took place at the Fairlane Inn near Ford World Headquarters. The group met 14 times and hatched a new frame of mind that they christened the

"Lively Ones." They conceived and approved a 1962 Falcon convertible and a sportier fastback called the Falcon Future with a vinyl roof and four-on-the-floor gearshift. The new small-block thin-wall V-8 would also go into another new Falcon model called the Sprint.

The Fairlane Committee had only begun. The Lively Ones evolved into the Total Performance theme, which code-named a multi-pronged attack aimed directly at General Motors and Chrysler, the two blatant rule-benders

Using a cut-down windshield to reduce wind resistance and weight was just one of the ways Shelby worked to make this 1964 289 Cobra competitive in the USRRC series.

A diagonal roll-bar brace bisected the cockpit, improving the 1964 USRRC 289 Cobra's structural rigidity. The Ford V-8 was set well back; the front of the block was behind the front wheels' centerline. *Randy Leffingwell*

Simple, clean, timeless. Shelby's melding of the A.C. body with the American V-8 engine resulted in one of the finest sports cars of the 1960s. *Randy Leffingwell*

The lack of air cleaners on a 1964 289 Cobra USRRC exemplifies the purpose-built nature of the brutal car. A diminutive windshield fulfilled the regulations, and little more. *Randy Leffingwell*

of the AMA performance ban. Henry Ford II had supported the ban but now felt embarrassed and betrayed by his competitors' shenanigans. Iacocca convinced him to confront the other two industry giants. After Chrysler and GM innocently denied wrongdoing, Ford began to quietly look for ways and means to return to racing.

In August 1961, Ford announced the sportier Falcon models and introduced the new small V-8. In September, Ray Brock's *Hot Rod* magazine and other enthusiast publications in England and the United States reported that Bristol would no longer provide engines for A.C.'s most popular sporting roadster. As far as Carroll Shelby's dream was concerned, Ford's new commitment to change its image comprised the third coincidence that affected him, and all of these swept in a serendipitous wave against his enforced retirement from racing. The *American Heritage Dictionary* defines "coincidence" as "A sequence of events that although accidental seems to have been planned or

arranged." If there were an illustration next to that dictionary entry, it would have to be Carroll Shelby's smiling face.

Shelby contacted Evans, who listened to the idea and agreed to send him a sample 221 V-8. The Texan borrowed a friend's A.C. Ace, pulled the Bristol 2-liter out and test-fitted the Ford engine. It appeared to be a straightforward replacement offering considerably better performance at a weight penalty of just a few pounds, so he then wrote to Charles Hurlock proposing a different V-8 (though it was still a Ford product). Hurlock was surprised by the inquiry, intrigued by the idea, and pleased at the prospect of saving part of his lineup. He agreed to try the idea. Shelby telephoned Dave Evans with Hurlock's response in early November and got more good news: Ford engineering had bored out the 221 to make 260 cubic inches, and this block was available for the Falcons. Evans promised to ship two more engines to Shelby, and he could send one of those to A.C. Cars in England.

Functional fender louvers vented engine-compartment heat, a concern in a high-powered car with a compact radiator. The fender badge discreetly announced what was under the hood, in case the exhaust note failed to do so.

Randy Leffingwell

A 1964 289 Cobra FIA lunges towards the apex of Turn 8A at Laguna Seca Raceway during the 2003 Monterey Historic Automobile Races. Only five FIA Cobras were built, using special carburetion, an aluminum T-10 four-speed transmission, and bulges on the trunk lid to allow a suitcase to fit—an FIA requirement. Notice the sophisticated trunk latch.

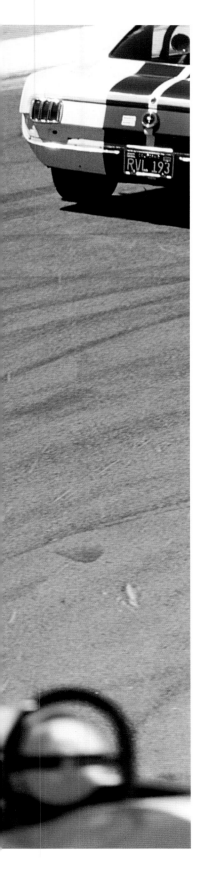

Shelby already had hired his first employee, Jean Sherman. He met her at Bill Harrah's casino where she was helping him establish his car museum in Reno. Carroll told her about his dream, and a couple months later she relocated to Santa Fe Springs.

Shelby's entrepreneurial spirit had taken off. His Le Mans victory benefited him when he founded the Shelby School of High Performance Driving in 1961. The school was a winner right from the starting flag: His first magazine ads drew more than a thousand responses. Shelby rented Riverside International Raceway east of Santa Fe Springs whenever enough wannabe racers got together the necessary fees and taught newbies about high-performance driving. To aid him in this venture, he added a second employee to run the school, an accomplished racer and even more accomplished car designer named Peter Brock (not related to journalist Ray Brock).

Peter Brock had worked at General Motors design, joining the styling staff as a 19-year-old in 1956. Within months of Brock's arrival at GM, design chief Bill Mitchell announced he wanted to do an all-new Corvette for 1960 based on what he'd just seen at the Turin Auto Show in Italy. Brock drew a sensuously undulating, boat-tailed coupe that got closest to what Mitchell had in mind. When Mitchell asked for a roadster version, Brock's friend Chuck Pohlmann completed that project. Corporate politics, however, especially as they elevated, side-tracked, or sunk projects outright in Bill Mitchell's styling studios, wore on Brock. He left, and Pohlmann and Mitchell's first lieutenant Larry Shinoda

completed the details of what became Chevrolet's striking 1963 Corvette Stingray. Brock, a graduate of Los Angeles' Art Center College of Design (now in Pasadena) returned to California and immersed himself in the hot-rod and racing scene where he met Shelby.

Just after New Year's in 1962, Charles Hurlock notified Shelby that he had a running prototype ready for Carroll's inspection. On a cold, rainy February 1, the retired racer walked onto England's Silverstone racetrack and inspected the bare metal car body cobbled together around Ford's little V-8. As he walked around it, he liked the way the car looked. When he started it and drove off, he liked the way its American V-8 engine sounded. As he drove, lap after lap, he liked the way it ran. He immediately found dozens of things to change, improve, or upgrade: The gearbox wasn't strong enough; the car needed more robust front spindles, bigger brakes, and a stiffer suspension. But he left England weeks later knowing that the Hurlocks and A.C. would change the things they could in California, he knew where to find the rest of what he needed. He left the engine with A.C. so they could begin to perfect the chassis modifications to manufacture the car more easily. Charles Hurlock agreed to ship another Ace (without engine) to Shelby in Santa Fe Springs so he, Dean Moon, and Peter Brock could assemble one there.

Soon after that Ace arrived, Moon and Shelby quickly married the other 260 V-8 engine to the A.C. body and chassis. They went out for a hard drive around the oil derricks that crowded Moon's shop. The car went faster and worked

A 1964 FIA 289 Cobra leads the 1963 Corvette originally driven by Bob Bondurant through the Corkscrew turn at Laguna Seca Raceway during the 2003 Monterey Historic Automobile Races. *Randy Leffingwell*

Fewer than 90 days passed from the start of construction of the first Cobra Daytona Coupe in October 1963 to its first track test. On March 21, 1964, it earned its first GT-class win and fourth overall at the 12 Hours of Sebring.

Brutally functional, the Cobra Coupe used a Kamm-inspired design at the rear to supply downforce by creating a low-pressure zone. The peerless proportions are evident when seen from this angle.

Penned by Pete Brock, the Cobra Daytona Coupe was designed to present the smallest frontal area possible while using race-proven Cobra components. Brock was an early proponent of utilizing aerodynamics in the design of race cars.

better than they had hoped. It never missed a beat or a turn through the dirt around the towers. Shelby called Dave Evans to let him know how well the car worked. Evans announced that it was time for Shelby to come to Dearborn, to meet the people who could move the project forward. Evans led the Texan to Don Frey and Jacque Passino. Because of his Le Mans win, Ford's

execs—especially Passino—had heard of Shelby and knew his reputation. However, when he reached Dearborn, Carroll talked about the cars he wanted to build and not his own accomplishments.

"It was simple," Shelby recalled. "I asked them to give me four engines and twenty-five thousand dollars and I'd built them a car that would put away the Corvette." That

Bred for the racetrack, Shelby's Cobra Daytona Coupe silenced many who thought that the quickly developed race car would fall on its face. The impressive record by the Shelby American Cobra team culminated at the Bonneville Salt Flats in November 1965, when a Daytona Coupe set 23 records and averaged 170 miles per hour for 12 hours. *Randy Leffingwell*

impressed Ford's decision makers. As Passino recalled, "Shelby walked in at just the right time and he told Frey and me that if we supplied him with a few engines, he would build a high-performance production sports car that would 'blow the pants off the Corvette!' Well, that was all we needed to hear. We got him his engines."

Knowing the financial risks in any factory-supported racing program, Shelby asked for an in-house "bean counter," an accountant to review every expenditure he made with Ford's money. Frey assigned Ray Geddes to serve as liaison between Ford and Carroll's newly formed company, Shelby American. Geddes, with a law degree and accounting background, had joined Ford the previous June 1961 in the comptroller's office. He had already started, run, and sold a business of his own. His small-business experience was much different from those who had joined

Side exhaust pipes were tucked into the rocker panels to reduce drag. Like the Cobra roadster, the driver sat immediately in front of the rear tires in an effort to balance the weight distribution. *Randy Leffingwell*

A 1965 Shelby Daytona Coupe sweeps past a 1963 Cobra at the top of Laguna Seca's Corkscrew during the 2003 Monterey Historic Automobile Races. The coupe was at home on high-speed circuits, while the roadster excelled on tight courses.

Ford directly from college. This, Frey believed, gave Geddes the perspective necessary to understand what should and should not happen when creating new business enterprises.

Shelby proposed building 100 identical cars to qualify the model for production racing against Chevrolet's Corvette. Geddes, as Frey's insider educated in Ford's ways of doing things, was empowered to keep things on time, on budget, and on the race tracks. Geddes was a logical, if unprepared, choice. "I wasn't a sports car enthusiast." He told Dave Friedman. "I'd never heard of Carroll Shelby. The only stick shift I'd ever driven was the 1937 Oldsmobile that my grandmother had," he recalled years later.

While Shelby had assembled his first Ford-powered A.C. at Dean Moon's shop, it was clear that if he were going to build 100 or more of them, he needed a place of his own. Lance Reventlow, heir to the Revlon cosmetic

An air box surrounded the four Weber carburetors bolted to a 289-cubic-inch V-8 in the 1965 Cobra Daytona Coupe. The foam on the perimeter of the air box fit against the bottom of the hood, allowing fresh, cool air from the hood scoop to be fed directly into the carb throats. *Randy Leffingwell*

Being pitched through a turn at Laguna Seca, a 1965 Shelby Daytona Coupe puts the right-side tires over the rumble strips as the power is fed to the rear tires. Plexiglas covers over the headlights help create a wind-cheating shape.

The large hole in the hood was designed to extract hot air from the radiator. Behind the opening sat the 289-cubic-inch V-8 engine. *Randy Leffingwell*

family fortune, had just forsaken his business of building racing cars in order to capture a world championship either in Formula One or sports cars, so his shops on L.A.'s west side in Venice were available. They came with most, but not all, of the equipment a race-car shop needed. Geddes arranged a further $20,000 in Ford "sponsorship" for the remaining equipment and went above and beyond his work negotiating a favorable price for the engines coming from Dearborn. Geddes traveled to Thames Ditton and solidified costs to Shelby American for A.C.'s cars and chassis. Shelby American was in business.

To this day, Shelby maintains the name for the car came to him in a dream. Whatever its origin, the story of the racing Cobras is one of the great legends of motor sports. While Carroll's first 260 V-8 Cobra didn't win in its debut against four new 1963 factory-race-prepared 360-horsepower 327-cubic-inch Z06 Corvette Stingray coupes, it put Chevrolet on notice immediately. Where Chevrolet apparently wanted only to win races in Chevrolet cars powered by Chevrolet engines, Ford seemed content, at least initially, to win races in vehicles "powered by Ford."

Billy Krause, who did most of the development driving at the Pomona race circuit to work the bugs out, campaigned the first Cobra 260 roadster against Chevrolet's Corvettes. He didn't finish the race. "As we did more and more testing at Riverside," Krause explained to another former Shelby employee, Dave Friedman, "it got better and better. By the time we ran our first race at Riverside in October 1962, that car was pretty damn good. I had a huge lead when the rear hub carrier broke and put us out of the race. We should have won, but the Cobra was a new car and things kept breaking." However that was just about the last time a Z06 won against a Cobra. Corvette's racing guru Zora Arkus-Duntov used the threat Shelby's Cobras posed to persuade Semon E. "Bunkie" Knudsen, Chevrolet

division's new general manager, into approving a more serious racing program consisting of Gran Sport Corvettes. Years later, Knudsen would find a way to get even with Shelby for his racing Cobras.

After Shelby completed assembly of the 75th car with Ford's 260 V-8, the new 289 Hi-Performance engines appeared. Those cars not only humbled GM's Chevrolet division but embarrassed race-car manufacturers all over the world, occasionally even the target Carroll Shelby sought most: Enzo Ferrari.

Recognizing that open cars were seldom as aerodynamically efficient as closed ones, Peter Brock designed a gorgeous if aerodynamically-challenged Cobra coupe for Daytona and other high-speed circuits in 1963. While Californian Peter Brock had provided one avenue to beat the Ferraris, the Texan, knowing that sometimes the solution to any problem was just to "get a bigger hammer," had a new Ford engine in mind.

This front-fender-mounted badge was the only external clue to what was lurking under the hood. The badge was from the very first Cobra.

Engine-cooling vents were installed in 1964, as seen on this 1965 289 Cobra. Unlike most of its sports-car contemporaries, Cobras utilized four-wheel disc brakes. Shelby had learned early in his racing career that stopping was as important as acceleration.

Like most automobiles in the early 1960s, bumpers were little more than decoration. Rarely was the soft top installed. Even rarer was the optional hardtop; few buyers sprang for it.

Externally, the Cobra roadster deviated little from its original A.C. Ace roots, with modest fender flares allowing larger tires to fit. The biggest difference was under the hood in the form of a small-block Ford V-8 engine.

In the finest English sports car tradition, knock-off wire wheels came standard on the Cobra 289. Occasional tightening of the spinner with a hide hammer eliminated the chance of a wheel becoming detached on the road.

Any proper sports car required full instrumentation, and the Cobra 289 carried a full set. The A.C. logo was retained on the horn button, as well as the pedals, as seen on this 1965 example. A large wooden steering wheel allowed the driver to get an upper-body workout during spirited driving; power steering depended on how strong the driver's arms were.

The 289 coupe debuted at Daytona in February 1964, the same day that Bob Bondurant test-drove Shelby's first 427-cubic-inch V-8-powered Cobra roadster at Riverside. Ken Miles and others in Shelby's shops had spotted a prototype 427 NASCAR engine on a pallet in the corner of the shop two months earlier in December. Someone had wondered aloud: What would happen if they put that into a Cobra?

And so the 427 Cobra was born. The car represented many things to many people. At Shelby, the car was known as "The Turd," for its ungainly appearance and unforgiving handling. At Ford, it was an opportunity for several engineers to prove the value of computer modeling in suspension

The Cobra utilized 22 panels to form the body. Shelby paid A.C. $1,500 for each rolling body/chassis.

Originally fitted with a 260-cubic-inch V-8 when it debuted in 1962, the Cobra roadster engine's displacement was bumped up to 289 cubic inches after the first 75 Cobras were built. The new engine delivered 271 horsepower.

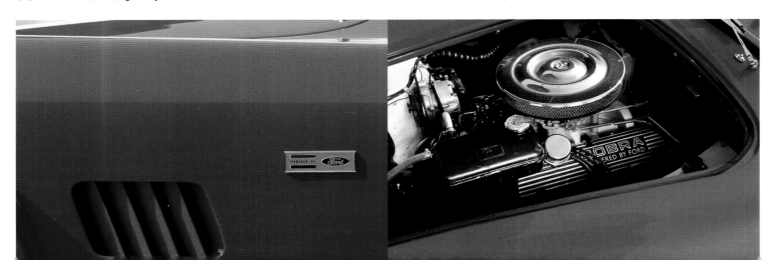

At the other end of this shifter was
a Borg-Warner all synchromesh manual
transmission. A reverse lock-out
prevented inadvertent gear selection;
reverse was engaged by lifting the
T-handle, then slipping the shifter into gear.

Cobra occupants enjoyed intimate seating,
thanks to an interior that was pure vintage
British sports car. This 1965 Cobra sold new
for approximately $5,995.

Above: **One of the wildest vehicles ever unleashed onto American roads, the 1965 427 Cobra used brute force in lieu of finesse. Ostensibly rated at 390 horsepower, it could generate 500-plus horsepower with ease. It was definitely not a car for beginners.**

Left: **This 1965 427 Cobra was a thinly disguised race car with a license plate. Sealed-beam headlights allowed the Cobra to be seen, period.**

design. Chassis engineers Bob Negstad and Klaus Arning, and Chuck Carrig, a FORTRAN computer language programmer from Ford's data-processing department, began working on the idea in 1961. By the time Shelby was ready to build the bigger hammer, Negstad was assigned to Ray Geddes, and Carrig was running numbers. It took a new chassis to handle the horsepower and torque of the engine and while it never was the most graceful of racers, if the 289s were successful, the 427s were indomitable.

Sometime early in 1964, Don Frey called on one of his product-planning staff. John Onken had written Ford's blue paper proposing a new four-passenger two-door model that would go into production in another six months as the Ford Mustang. This internal document described the new product as a "secretary's car that men would enjoy driving." The paper laid out general dimensions, probable department involvement, estimated time frames, proposed costs, suggested marketing and advertising strategies, and

Above: Unwary occupants stood a good chance of searing their legs on the huge exhaust pipes, and the exhaust note played havoc with their hearing. The roll bar provided a modicum of protection in case of a rollover, but most drivers didn't worry.

Right: With the huge 427-cubic-inch engine in the bow, rapid handling was not the big-block Cobra's forte. It was more at home on a long straight stretch, where the brutish engine could wind up.

An aluminum air box surrounded the 780-cubic-foot-per-minute Holley four-barrel carburetor on the 1965 427 Cobra as a method of reducing the amount of underhood heat soak to the carb. The functional hood scoop directed ambient air to the air cleaner.

Safety wiring the knock-off spinners was an easy way to prevent a wheel departure at speed.

Cobra's engine compartment. Routine maintenance was a challenge, as access to some of the spark plugs was compromised. A 14-quart dry-sump oil system helped keep engine temperatures below the meltdown point.

potential sales against other Ford products and outside competitors. In this blue paper, Onken had recommended, and Frey had approved, a number of performance options for the Mustang in keeping with Ford's new performance orientation. John knew his way around the engine engineering department, having worked with them on regular production 289 high-performance power plants for Falcons, Fairlanes, and the coming Mustang. Frey stood at his door with a sheaf of papers.

"Have you seen this? Is there anything we can do about it?" Frey asked. Onken recognized the papers his boss was holding.

"We're losing three hundred dollars on each of those engines we're selling that fellow Shelby for his Cobras!" Frey explained. Those engines were the company's new 427-cubic-inch-displacement V-8s in the Cobras. Ford's

engine division personnel hand assembled each engine. Both men understood that the company's contract that Geddes had negotiated allowed no price adjustment until its terms had expired.

Onken offered to make a few calls to friends in engineering and then report back to his boss. It took a few hours and he had hatched a solution. Onken called Frey and then went over to his office at world headquarters. "We can make it a regular production option," Onken told Frey. "Give it an RPO code, the '427 R' or something, and they'll put it together on an assembly line. It won't hurt the performance but it lowers our costs by two hundred forty dollars per unit."

"So now we're losing only sixty dollars on each one?" Frey asked. "Well, someday, we'll have to find a way for Mr. Shelby to pay us back for this favor."

Voluptuous fenders had grown dramatically to cover the ever-growing tires, which were necessary as increasingly powerful engines were slipped in. The dog-leg shifter was necessary due to the rearward installation of the engine/transmission package.

Above: The large tachometer was located directly in front of the driver, while the speedometer was mounted just to the left of center. Notice how the speedometer swings counterclockwise.

Right: The purity of the original A.C. design was still evident after the huge 427-cubic-inch V-8 was shoehorned into the engine compartment. Massive power in a 2,100-pound package tends to grab a driver's attention. On racetracks around the world, it was victorious.

Below: With the proper use of throttle, clutch, shifter, and disc brakes, it was possible to accelerate from 0–100 miles per hour and back to 0 in 14 seconds.

CHAPTER TWO

HOME FROM EUROPE TO TURN THE MUSTANG INTO A RACER: 1964-1965

Left: The 1965 GT350 came in any color as long as it was Wimbledon White with Guardsman Blue lower-body stripes. Few external modifications were done, as most of the changes were under the sheet metal.

Below: Optional 6x15-inch two-piece wheels, an aluminum center surrounded by a steel rim, were built by Cragar. The exhaust pipes dumping in front of the rear tires would last only through the 1965 model year.

Above left: **Narrow 7.75x15 Goodyear Blue Dot tires were no match for the 306-horsepower 289-cubic-inch V-8. An aluminum Cobra oil pan can be seen beneath the engine.**

FORD'S NEW MUSTANG IMMEDIATELY INTRIGUED RACERS. In Detroit, they moved quickly. Bob Acton, a plumbing company owner on Telegraph Road between 6-Mile and 7-Mile, bought a 1964 1/2 pumpkin-orange notchback and began to campaign it at Waterford Hills soon after the cars first went on sale. Joe Mulholland, a Ford engineer, raced an aluminum-bodied XKE roadster on weekends against Acton and a group of Corvettes at Waterford, where he held the class lap record. He had watched the Mustang come together, from the engine and chassis guys who made the two-seat mid-engine model to the product planners, stylists, engineers, and production people who turned out this new hardtop.

Mulholland kept looking at the cars and thinking about them. He saw the car's shortcomings. It only had a three-speed manual transmission. It only had drum brakes. It only had a commuter's suspension. It only had narrow, bias-ply tires. It only had, in its most basic configuration, a 101-horsepower 170-cubic-inch inline six-cylinder engine. But Mulholland and nearly everyone else knew this was a strategic decision to keep the car at a low introductory price. Anyone interested in performance could order the 164-horsepower F-code 260 Challenger V-8 or the 210-horsepower 289-cubic-inch D-code engine and wait

Above: **Koni shock absorbers at each corner and lowered front upper A-arms gave the 1965 Shelby GT350 handling prowess that a stock Mustang couldn't touch. Override traction bars required that holes be cut into the floor of the vehicle, then boots were installed to keep dust and noise from seeping into the interior.**

Left: **Early production 1965 GT350s did not have an identification badge inboard of the right taillight. Note the use of the stock Mustang gas cap.**

Tri-element taillights have been a Mustang, and Shelby Mustang, styling cue from day one. Early production GT350s had a trunk-mounted battery, but after complaints of fumes wafting into the cockpit, the battery was moved under the hood.

The Mustang's galloping horse was deleted from the 1965 Shelby GT350, replaced with the small badge from the Mustang's front fender. The stylized C-scoop was meant to visually tie the Mustang to the original 1962 Mustang I.

patiently for delivery. The A-code 225-horsepower and K-code 271-horsepower high-performance versions appeared as regular production options for 1965 models in late 1964. Mulholland knew they were coming and he was aware that inside Ford's parts warehouses (and already options for some of the company's other models) were the rest of the bits he and Ford would need to make the Mustang a real racer. But how could he get the company to build him a production racer so he wasn't competing as a modified car against higher classes and prototypes?

Mulholland had no idea how many allies he had who were already working on that very question. In Europe, Ford had achieved some notoriety with its production-based cars: Galaxies and Falcons initially in 1963 and pre-production Mustangs in early 1964. These cars ran in poorly veiled races held over open roads. Walter Hayes, vice president of public affairs for Ford of Europe, and Walter Murphy, Ford's

advertising account executive at J. Walter Thompson, had launched the company's international racing efforts in January 1963 with several race-prepared Falcons. One of them accomplished the best times over six icy stages of the grueling 4,000-mile Monte Carlo Rally. The Monte comprises many more than six stages and only one Falcon completed the rally, coming in 34th overall out of 296 starters and 96 cars that finished the event.

Frank Zimmerman, Lee Iacocca's special vehicles manager, understood that race-car development took time. Later that year, Zimmerman entered several Galaxies in the Tour de France de l'Automobile, a high-speed sprint over open roads connecting several timed events contested on race circuits. Ford earned no outright victories in 1963, but undiscouraged, they committed a much larger effort for 1964, beginning with the January Monte Carlo Rally. Ford Division entered eight Falcon Futura Sprints. A separate

Starting with the 271-horsepower, K-code, 289-cubic-inch V-8, Shelby fitted a cast-aluminum Hi-Riser intake manifold and a 715-cubic-foot-per-minute Holley four-barrel carburetor to help the small-block breathe. He opened up the exhaust system by bolting on Tri-Y steel headers and Glaspak mufflers. The result was 306 horsepower.

Bob Bondurant slides the Ford GT40 during one of the many tests run at Riverside between late December 1964 and late January 1965. It was during this eight-week period that the Shelby teams turned this car into the overall winner at Daytona in February 1965. That was the first win for the GT40 after a disastrous debut season in 1964.

David Friedman collection

team from Ford of England and Alan Mann Racing registered four not-yet-introduced Mustangs fitted with prototype K-code V-8s. John Holman at Holman Moody's North Carolina race shop tweaked the engines out to 285 horsepower.

Holman's work delayed the cars' delivery to England. Mann's shops had no time to reinforce the bodies and chassis as they had done to the Falcons, but the cars got stiffer and stronger front coil and rear leaf springs and shock absorbers. Mann mounted Girling front disc brakes as well. While the 1963 rally had been contested in snow and ice, the weather during the 1964 running gave competitors dry pavements that favored the powerful Fords with their high top speeds and the nimble and maneuverable Mini Coopers.

Typically the Monte Carlo Rally starts from several locations throughout Europe, and in 1964, 299 contestants

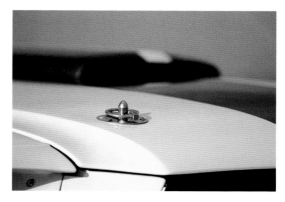

Making the hood out of fiberglass allowed the incorporation of a functional hood scoop. Locking Klik pins kept the hood in place and imparted an authentic race-car look.

Tidy dimensions are a hallmark of 1960s-era British sports cars, and the Sunbeam Tiger, built from the four-cylinder Alpine, fit the mold. Standard Tigers packed 164 horsepower under the hood; the 1964 Targa Florio Tiger used a Shelby-massaged engine to stuff close to 300 horsepower into the diminutive racer. *Randy Leffingwell*

began in nine cities on January 17. Entrants converged on Monaco, finishing there after 1,550 kilometers (about 970 miles) on January 24. One of the Falcons finished 2nd overall behind a Mini Cooper and 1st in class, with the others following at 11th, 19th, 39th and on out from there. None of the three notchback Mustangs finished (though Mann's other entries, compact Ford Cortinas with Lotus cylinder heads on four-cylinder engines, ranked 22nd, 24th, and 26th out of 164 finishers). To the French, who were fans of Ford cars and encouraged the company's participation in motor sports, a class win meant as much as overall victory. But for Lee Iacocca and the other Fairlane Committee regulars, they needed successful performance closer to home to drive American customers into local dealers.

How Fords went racing and how they won did not concern the division manager; Iacocca had engineers on staff as well as an outsider named Carroll Shelby who could reason it through and work it out. Iacocca had a vision for Ford products. He wanted to make cars not only more sporting than Robert McNamara's Falcon, but

also more sophisticated. Although Iacocca had little direct contact with Europe's most exotic cars, they embodied the refinement he wanted, especially Ferrari. He and Don Frey occasionally had discussed this perspective and they idly had considered making overtures to Ferrari. What's more, Henry Ford II was upset with General Motor's consistent flaunting of the A.M.A. racing ban. Henry had decided not only to beat them in the U.S. but to take on all competition worldwide. With Henry Ford II's blessing, Frey followed this idea through during early 1963. By May, however, as Ferrari pressed for one concession after another the deal collapsed. This inflamed Henry Ford II, and Iacocca and Frey—who had led the final round of negotiations—reacted quickly. Within days, Iacocca inaugurated a plan for Ford's own program of GT40 racers.

Unsure of how to proceed with his own desires to take the new Mustang racing, Ford engineer Joe Mulholland called his product planner friend John Onken and leveled with him. It was early in the summer of 1964. Onken knew that Australian racer Allan Moffat was in

Dearborn working with Ford Engineering to establish a racing program in the United States for the Ford-Lotus Cortinas that Alan Mann had campaigned in Europe. As Onken contemplated the task ahead of him, he knew Mulholland had his own ideas, but Onken reasoned that getting a second opinion on the Mustang might be valuable. While he knew of Ford's growing participation in competition, he didn't know how he could disguise a race car if management wasn't ready for this particular one.

A few days later, Onken, Mulholland, and Moffat headed up to Waterford with two production notchbacks. As Onken recalled it, the drivers went off the track everywhere. The tight 1.5-mile 13-turn course favors smaller cars like Moffat's Cortinas and it severely challenged the Mustangs. (Within weeks, Moffat would claim his own class lap record in a Cortina.) Waterford's 1,000-foot-long back straightaway ends in a 90-degree right turn with little run-off before reaching the edge of the racing club property. Paddock Turn is a 180-degree right-hander that is, like much of the track, flat and deceptively tight. Every corner at Waterford has an increasing-radius, so racers accelerate hard from the apex on. Moffat and Mulholland used up tires, brakes, and clutches, and they nearly cooked the cars. A few of the track regulars were out to watch that day. Anne Roeske and Jerry Marlewski each recalled that, by the end of the afternoon,

This 1964 Sunbeam Tiger ran the 1965 Targa Florio race, piloted by Peter Harper and the Reverend Rupert Jones. Shelby's engineers helped build the first of this hybrid, having some experience in installing small-block Ford V-8 engines into small British sports cars. *Randy Leffingwell*

Above: A "works" rally car, this 1964 Sunbeam Tiger was built by the Rootes Racing Department, and finished second in the prototype class in the 1965 Targa Florio, behind a Ferrari 275P2. A 3.55:1 rear-axle ratio helped keep the 289-cubic-inch Ford engine in its powerband. *Randy Leffingwell*

In order to prevent overheating of the 4.7-liter Ford V-8, the 1964 Targo Floria Sunbeam Tiger race car had the largest possible grille opening, as well as a bulging fiberglass hood to clear the engine. *Randy Leffingwell*

idea was the question that nagged at him.

Overnight it struck him. Through the late 1950s, Ford had been the "safe" car company. The Edsel, despite its shortcomings, had introduced self-adjusting brakes and stronger steel wheel rims, among other features. Back at his office the next day, Onken prepared a blue paper for a new, safer Mustang. Both Mann and Mulholland had criticized the loose, sloppy steering. To "improve evasive maneuvering," Onken called for the stiffer springs, shock absorbers, and bushings that Ford had used on the Monte Carlo Falcons and Mustangs. He specified the Wide Oval 70-series tires that other planners scheduled to appear on Ford products. A different steering linkage or gearbox might make turn-in more responsive. The Thunderbird had front disc brakes, useful on his new Mustang for safer stopping. For better cooling and longer drivetrain life, he knew Ford's truck division had big radiators and heavy-duty clutches.

the two cars were completely spent and steaming, and the two racers with vastly different ideas of how to convert a passenger production road car into a racer were steaming as well. They did agree that the car needed a four-speed transmission, front disc brakes, better tires, a stiffer suspension, better cooling, quicker steering, a heavy-duty clutch, and, somehow, better balance.

Onken had authored the initial blue paper to Don Frey that created the Mustang. Iacocca's assignment still rang in his ears: A car for the ladies, but one that the men would enjoy driving. Now Onken had to convince Frey and Iacocca that men should enjoy driving the new car fast! He could navigate his way around the product development system. More than that, Onken knew from specifying them where Mustang parts would originate. But how he sold the

It cost only $4,547 to put a brand-new 1965 Shelby GT350 in your driveway. It could cover the quarter mile in 15.7 seconds at 91 miles per hour. Zero to 60 miles per hour needed 7.0 seconds, while 60–0 needed 140 feet.

The balance question was tougher, but the answer came from an unanticipated design change. As the notchback underwent final development, stylists had prepared an unauthorized fastback as a 2 + 2. When Iacocca saw it, he rushed it into production for the fall. Engineers had assured Onken that the large rear window on the 2 + 2 added weight on the back end of the car. Problem solved.

On paper, Onken described the purpose of the car as a safer, more durable Mustang. He put the proposal into interoffice mail and awaited the inevitable conversation with his boss, Don Frey.

At the same time, Frey and his boss Lee Iacocca knew from Ford dealer reports that sales personnel liked having Shelby Cobras in their showrooms. It generated excitement that drew in traffic. Frey had assigned Ray Geddes to shepherd a new program to perpetuate dealer enthusiasm— and get the Mustang qualified as a racer. Iacocca had asked Frey to keep the Shelby performance dealer network together and he wanted Shelby involved.

When Onken got to Don Frey's office, the professorial division vice president and head of planning was far ahead of him. Frey knew Plymouth had engineering and handling improvements ready for the new Barracuda. He had solid information that Chevrolet had its own "Mustang" for 1967. Good competition, he recognized, induced better sales for everybody. Frey's job was to ensure that competitive advantages remained on Ford's side.

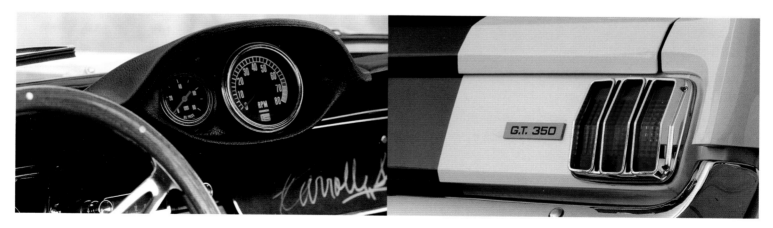

In order to minimize the distance a driver's eyes had to deviate from watching the road, Shelby installed the tachometer and oil pressure gauge in a binnacle atop the dashboard. Falling oil pressure was often the first sign a driver had that conditions under the hood were going south.

Shelby did not have a massive budget, or a lot of time, to put the 1965 GT350 into production, so exterior modifications were held to a minimum. The addition of a small badge and full-length stripes were the only visual clues when looking at the rear of the vehicle.

Above: Only 36 R-model GT350s were built in 1965, and all were intended just for track use. Only two were Shelby Team racers, including this one, 5R102. Shelby pointed out that the interior was "fireproof," another way to say gutted.

Left: A fiberglass front lower apron replaced the bumper and directed air through the radiator and oil cooler. The holes outboard of the center opening fed cooling air to the front brakes.

He had been Henry Ford II's point man with Ferrari a year earlier but he came home empty-handed. In lieu of buying their success, now Ford encouraged the racing programs that sprouted up everywhere—from European GTs to Shelby's Cobras to open-wheeled Ford-powered Lotus racers at the Indy 500. John Onken's idea was posited as a safety measure, and now here was one of Frey's own planners fielding a thinly disguised proposal for something already on Frey's horizon as an approaching target.

"So, you're building a racing Mustang, are you? How do you plan to make it work? Who have you got involved?" Frey asked.

Onken explained the previous day's work at Waterford and the heated disagreement between the two racers. Frey stared at the paper for a long moment. Then he looked at Onken.

"Well, he turned that little English sports car into a race winner. He's beating Ferrari in Europe. His cars are beating Corvettes here. Maybe it's time to call Mr. Shelby in to repay the favor we've been giving him with his Cobra engines."

It was July before Frey could meet with Shelby. Le Mans had come and gone. Ford had hastily created three GT40s that looked good and went fast until they slowed

All 1,065 GT350Rs came with 15x7-inch magnesium wheels in an effort to reduce weight. R models were 300 pounds lighter than standard GT350s, which is one of the reasons they went on to dominate the B-Production class.

Removing the rear bumper and replacing the back window with Plexiglas shaved pounds from the 1965 GT350R. Side windows were also Plexiglas and were raised by pulling a leather strap; the window regulators were tossed to save weight.

and pulled off. Two retired with broken gearboxes before dawn, while the third had burned up after 5 hours' running. Nineteen sixty-four Ferraris took first, second, and third, with one of Shelby's 4.7-liter Cobra Coupes coming in fourth.

Shelby had heard that Ford intended to give him responsibility for ongoing GT40 development programs to make them winners. He was planning to collaborate with Dan Gurney in a joint Indy race effort for 1965 and create a new company together. There were suggestions that he put the Cobra coupe into limited production as the Ford Cobra GT. He still had unsold 427 Cobras parked behind his shops.

Obligations pulled Shelby in several directions at once. While he had no desire to bite the hand that fed him, he also didn't want to fail in front of his masters. Leo Beebe took the position as special vehicles manager from Frank Zimmerman in April, before Le Mans. Henry Ford II

had assigned Beebe to win Indianapolis, Le Mans, and Daytona. And here was Shelby, ever more involved with Beebe's big three, and yet Don Frey and Lee Iacocca, the men who had made everything possible, now wanted more.

Jacque Passino had assigned John Cowley to look into Sports Car Club of America (SCCA) certification for the Mustang as a production sports car. Within weeks it was clear that Cowley was getting nowhere with John Bishop, executive director of the SCCA. Shelby, his arm twisted, agreed to intervene, and he learned from Bishop what he already knew from his Cobra enterprise. To qualify for production classes, the car had to be a two-seater. Manufacturers could modify either the suspension or the engine for racing purposes, but not both. Bishop's inspectors needed to examine 100 identical cars completed by January 1, 1965, for eligibility to race in that year. Bishop could not envision Shelby or Ford Motor Company producing so many race cars in barely five months.

51

Built to blur pavement, the 1965 GT350R cost about twice the price of a standard Mustang, but it delivered on the promises Shelby made. This R-model, 5R102, has been registered for street use, and the owner says that earplugs are mandatory above 4,000 rpm.

"When that happened," Shelby explained, "Iacocca called me and said, "Shelby, I want to make a high-perform-ance version of the Mustang. What you you have to do?"

Shelby knew he could do it but he also knew he didn't want to take it on. He had attended several of the introductions with Iacocca and he had gotten to know what the car was.

"That's a six cylinder car," he told Iacocca, "a secretary's car with a three-speed gearbox. That'd cost a lot of money," he went on.

"How much?"

He knew that Mustang sales had forced Ford to add production at Metuchen, New Jersey, and then San Jose, California, to the production at the Dearborn assembly plant already manufacturing the cars. San Jose was only 400 miles from his facilities near Los Angeles. That facility routinely turned out half of Bishop's 100-car requirement each day.

"I told him, 'It'd cost fifteen thousand dollars.'

"'You got it,' Iacocca said, and they sent me two cars to work on. Then a few days later Ray Geddes called me up and told me the bean counters had looked at the deal and changed things. All we have is fifteen hundred dollars. That's all.

"So I went to Goodyear and got five thousand dollars and I went to Castrol and got another five thousand. And that's where the first GT350 came from. Ford didn't even pay for it."

Shelby held two other advantages as well: Phil Remington and Ken Miles. Remington called himself a mechanic, perhaps because he was self-conscious about lacking a college degree. Semantics aside, Remington was an engineering and mechanical talent of probable-genius proportion. He had worked for Lance Reventlow on his Scarab racing project for five years, and when Reventlow quit and made his shops available, Carroll Shelby made sure Remington came with the lease. Ken Miles was an erudite and sometimes-arrogant Englishman, obsessively fit, and endowed with a cynical, wry sense of humor and driving skills that matched Remington's engineering abilities. Miles established many of the legends that still surround racing Cobras and GT40s to this day. He had become Shelby's competition director, staff racer, and chief development driver.

Shelby concluded that he could modify suspensions on a Mustang racer and sell a car that he could warranty against failures. Engines, he knew, were, well, engines. To some racers, test drivers, and magazine editors, they were meant to be blown up. Reluctantly, Shelby told Frey that he'd make the Mustang a racer. His own plan called for producing 100 "competition" cars and then assembling street versions. Within days, Frank Zimmerman released a

statement from Ford's Competition Department. It said that "One hundred lucky buyers" could purchase a Mustang with an independent rear suspension similar to what Ford raced on its new GT40 at Le Mans in 1964. Carroll Shelby, Zimmerman's release continued, would produce and race these cars just as he had done with his Cobras. The release then boasted that these new "Cobra-Mustangs" would follow their namesakes across the finish line, "second to Cobras and ahead of the Sting Rays."

Iacocca had Frey deliver the notchbacks to Venice, where Shelby began to make them race ready. Ken Miles and Phil Remington took them to Riverside International Raceway to evaluate the car and devise a plan for it. Their conclusions were discouraging. Even with Thunderbird discs up front, the brakes quickly faded to almost nothing. The 210-horsepower engine was desperately weak and its carburetor stalled the engine in the corners.

Shelby and Remington scoured Ford special parts catalogs, finding items for police cars and NASCAR racers that would improve the car. Shelby knew it wouldn't take much, perhaps $500 in parts billed internally as his engines had been, and he *could* transform the Mustang into a winner.

Herb Misch, Ford's chief of engineering, and the man who authorized the creation of the mid-engine Mustang I, followed through on Zimmerman's promise of an independent rear suspension, called an IRS. Roy Lunn's chassis and suspension engineer on Mustang I and the GT40 was Bob Negstad. He was the "greasy bits" guy who collaborated with FORTRAN programmer Chuck Carrig to create computer suspension designs for Shelby's 427 Cobras along with Dearborn-based Klaus Arning. Temporarily reassigned back to Dearborn from England and the GT40s, Negstad and Carrig contrived an IRS for the Mustang. Engineering fabricated two prototypes. One went directly to Shelby for evaluation.

By that time, however, Miles and Remington had devised their own solution to Mustang handling problems. Shelby had been specific: Create a car to hold on to a race

Left: Clips on the side of the rear window helped to hold it in place during high speeds when the cockpit became pressurized. The vent at the top of the rear window helped reduce this phenomenon.

track without getting so stiff they couldn't drive it on public streets. The modification should use parts readily available within Ford's main stream to keep the selling price reasonable. (By this time, Ford's "bean counters" had determined that it would cost $85,000 to design and develop Arning's IRS for the Mustang, much more than the $15,000 that Iacocca had "budgeted.") Arning came out from Dearborn. Together with Miles, Shelby team-co-driver Bob Bondurant, and Phil Remington, the group dialed in the Mustang's handling.

Miles and Arning lowered the front wheel upper control arms' inner pivot mount by 1 inch, essentially pre-compressing the suspension. To do this, Arning drilled new mounting holes in the wheel well. Original settings allowed front tires to roll under the car during hard cornering. The lower position forced the tires to remain upright, giving them more bite, which increased cornering power.

Mustang engineers had anticipated the inclinations of high-performance buyers and specified a 9-inch-diameter ring gear in the rear end on any order for the 225-horsepower or 271-horsepower V-8s. To keep their rear axles on the ground, Arning and Miles supplemented stiffer springs with drag-racing-type rear-axle traction bars. Ford's solid axle hopped under full-throttle acceleration or hard braking, and these bars limited that axle movement. The bars that straddled the top of the rear axle were too long to fit into the available rear-axle cavity, so Arning and Shelby mechanics cut slots through the floorpan and attached the forward end of the bars inside the car. This intruded into rear passenger seat room, but Shelby had removed the seats to meet SCCA racing regulations, defining Cobra-Mustangs as strictly two-seaters. Shelby fitted rubber boots over the bars to reduce road dirt and noise.

Anticipating the hard life of racing cars, Arning and Miles added safety cables to limit rear-axle drop if the car got airborne after a bump. These restrained the axle from falling too far and destroying the Koni adjustable shock absorbers that Miles installed. Shelby found that Ford's strongest rear axle and biggest rear brakes came on the Galaxie station wagon configured for heavy-duty towing. Surprisingly, it all fit easily on the Mustang. Arning and Miles replaced the 0.84-inch-diameter rear anti-sway bar with another that was 1 inch in diameter. To further stiffen the car, Arning adopted a cross-engine brace that he had seen on Alan Mann's Monte Carlo Rally Falcons. Listed in parts books as the "export brace," it spanned the engine compartment from right fender to left. Another bracket triangulated support from the shock-absorber towers to the firewall.

Inside the car, Miles and Remington gutted everything that added weight but didn't contribute to speed or safety. They replaced Ford's deeply dished plastic steering wheel with a flatter wood-rimmed version, allowing a straight-arm driving style. But it lacked the center horn button. Remington fabricated an on-dash button. He replaced Ford's production seatbelts with SCCA-approved 3-inch belts and shoulder harnesses connected by a large quick-release steel latch. Shelby deleted radios, reasoning that racers didn't need them and street customers couldn't hear them.

Ford's engineers gave the K-code 289-cubic-inch-displacement V-8 a stronger crankshaft and connecting rods as well as a dual-breaker-point distributor similar to what Shelby used on his Cobras. He replaced the starvation-prone Autolite carburetor with a Holley four-barrel 715-cubic-feet-per-minute model mounted on a new aluminum high-rise intake manifold that vaporized gasoline and air more completely. The Holley used a center pivot float that didn't hang up during Miles' hard-cornering evaluations. Remington discarded the factory exhaust and fit locally made steel headers to short pipes. Glass Pack mufflers finished the system. Remington's system got the exhaust out in the shortest possible distance from the engine while still remaining legal for racing. That put it, and the noise, just ahead of the rear tires. He also replaced the camshaft with another computer-designed improvement providing higher valve lift and longer opening duration. With the improved breathing and exhaust,

Shelby tweaked the GT350R's engine, balancing and blueprinting it to generate more power as well as enabling it to survive the rigors of competition. A purpose-built camshaft came alive at upper rpms, where the bulk of the engine's 360 horsepower lived.

Shelby's engine dynamometer tests revealed 306 brake horsepower at 6,000 rpm and 329 foot-pounds of torque at 4,200 rpm. To keep the engine lubricated, Remington enlarged oil capacity 30 percent, from 5 to 6.5 quarts of oil using a deeper baffled oil pan. Shelby finished the engine with finned, sand-cast aluminum valve covers embossed with the words "Cobra Powered by Ford."

Braking was no longer a problem by the time Miles, Remington, and co-development driver and team racer Bob Bondurant finished with the car. Kelsey-Hayes 11-inch-diameter discs replaced the inadequate Thunderbird units, and Remington put 2.5-inch-wide sintered metallic linings into the towing package's 10-inch rear drums. Appropriately, Shelby provided Goodyear Blue Dot 7.75x15-

To fit the wheel/tire package, the wheel openings were slightly flared and enlarged to provide clearance. The trunk held a 34-gallon fuel tank that was built up by welding two Mustang tanks together. A quick-fill gas cap was in the trunk, requiring opening of the trunk to fill the tank.

inch tires mounted on optional Cragar 6x15 wheels.

As this package neared completion, Shelby received his first three 2 + 2 fastback bodies from the San Jose plant. He prepared two of them, one using the Miles/Remington/Arning solid-axle traction-bar suspension and the other with the Arning/Negstad prototype IRS. Miles, Bondurant, and others flailed the cars around Willow Springs for hours before concluding that the more expensive IRS offered no additional benefit over what they had built. That was a decision—and a configuration—that influenced Mustang suspension design for decades to come.

Soon after Shelby moved his operation to Venice, California, he promoted Peter Brock from manager of the driving school to manager of special projects. When Ford's styling department dropped the idea of a Cobra-Mustang body, Shelby asked Brock to tackle matters of appearance. Peter had designed the Cobra head and Carroll's own CS logo, and he had conceived the blue-body/twin-white-stripe motif of the Cobras. Brock had long admired Briggs Cunningham's cars, and for the Mustangs, he adopted Cunningham's American racing color scheme using white

bodies and twin wide blue stripes. Brock also added the distinctive parallel lines and model designation along the rocker panels.

For weeks, Brock labored over a new logo. The Cobra-Mustang concept plagued him. During one of several discussions that Shelby had with Miles, Remington, Brock, and Ford personnel, the subject again came around to what the new car should be called. Ray Geddes explained that car model names required legal approval and formal registration. Using engine designations for car names was fine, they agreed, until specifications changed—and the stamped badges and printed material became obsolete. Numbers that weren't tied to anything, however, could be changed or upgraded whenever a manufacturer chose. A number that suggested more than it revealed was ideal. The model could continue for several years, receiving constant upgrades, without alerting sanctioning bodies. Shelby, anxious to get the matter settled, asked Remington to estimate the distance from their conference room to the shops across the street.

Everyone made their guesses and Remington paced it

off. He came back and announced it at 350 feet. "Fine," Shelby said. "Let's call the little car the GT350. If the car's good, the name won't matter, and if it's no good, the name won't matter."

Brock designed the supplemental instrument pod for the 8,000-rpm Delco tachometer and an oil-pressure gauge. A new instrument panel from Ford would take three years to reach production. Shelby needed 100 of them in three months, and Brock's tachometer sat closer to a racer's line of sight than Ford's dashboard. To get those 100 cars, Shelby took two full days of San Jose production. His cars came off the line in white with 289 K-code engines and basic black interiors that deleted the flip-up back seat.

Shelby ordered 15 more cars, stripped even further than his first 100. They arrived without rear- or side-window glass, interiors, insulation, headliners, heaters, defrosters, or gas tanks. While his growing staff started quickly on the 100 cars, work proceeded more deliberately on these 15. They were to be Shelby's first racers.

For two years, Remington and his crew had charmed a reliable 385 brake horsepower out of the 289 Cobra engine for racing purposes, even when detuned to last through endurance events. For the GT350 race cars, they dismantled San Jose's engines and sent the heads out to have intake and exhaust valve ports enlarged and polished. Remington's staff balanced every reciprocating piece from pistons to camshafts, and mechanics reassembled everything to blueprint specifications. Shelby and Remington conservatively estimated that the GT350R models developed 350 to 360 horsepower.

These new Rs weighed 250 pounds less than street cars. SCCA rules permitted Shelby American to remove the front and rear bumpers. Brock designed a cutaway front fiberglass piece into which Remington's mechanics sliced a large lip to better direct airflow through an oil cooler and radiator. Other holes on each side of the lip led cooling air to the front brake discs. Brock covered the side vents on the 2 + 2 roof that had disturbed laminar airflow. His one-

piece fiberglass hood had clips to hold it in place on both racing cars and, for the first time ever, on street cars.

When SCCA inspectors arrived at Shelby American's shops in late October, they found more than 100 GT350s. Some of Shelby's fifteen pure racers still sat in the garage. In preparation for the inspection, his staff had parked completed cars in tidy rows with numbered slots. *Competition Press & AutoWeek* magazine published a brief story on November 4, 1964, that SCCA had homologated the "Mustang-Cobra for Class B production" for 1965. The magazine had no photo. Corvette racers who already had reckoned with Shelby's Cobras could only wonder what the Texan had created for them now.

Remington completed the first two GT350R race cars for their February 1965 debut. Because Shelby American had satisfactorily assembled 100 models each with identical suspensions, Shelby was now free to modify his racing engines as he pleased. After Jerry Titus's track test appeared in *Sports Car Graphic* (SCG) in March 1965, orders began. (Titus had designed a tube frame for one of Shelby's Maserati racers in chalk on a garage floor in New York City a decade earlier. A skeptical Shelby took the car up to Lime Rock to test it and promptly set a lap record and their mutual respect and deep friendship began. Titus moved to California soon after Shelby arrived from Texas.)

Shelby's first two race cars remained his own "factory" entries. The next 13, completed within weeks, sold quickly. Carroll provided his customers with thorough updates and preparation tips. He knew other "official" teams engendered ill will with customers who felt they never could win against the factory, and he wanted none of that. For Ford and therefore for Shelby it was important only that a Mustang won. And win they did. The GT350Rs, with their distinctive ventilated Plexiglas rear window, established the same kind of near-invincibility that Shelby's Cobras had achieved. Mustangs, in particular one that *SCG*'s Titus drove for Shelby, grabbed the SCCA B-production class championship in 1965.

One of the 1965 GT350R models that Shelby used at his racing school approaches Turn 8A at the Monterey Historic Automobile Races. Despite the rarity and value of these Shelby Mustangs, many are enthusiastically driven at vintage events.

Shelby sold the R models for $5,995 and street versions went for $4,547. In 1965, he produced 515 road models and 35 competition versions in addition to three prototypes. Because drag racing still carried a broader national appeal than sports car racing, Shelby American worked with Bill Stroppe in Long Beach to assemble nine drag racers. Stroppe had gained considerable experience building several Fairlane 427 Thunderbolts. His engine builders replaced the San Jose engine valves with 1.625-inch-diameter exhaust valves and 1.875-inch intake valves, stronger valve springs, and simple drag exhaust headers. His mechanics installed front shocks with 90-10 lock-ups and the rears with 50-50 setting to improve weight transfer. Just before shipment, Stroppe placed an engine scatter shield, a drag-racing clutch, and a pressure plate in the trunk of each car for buyers to install themselves.

As the 1966 model year approached, Shelby began experimenting with ways to make his cars stand out. Remington installed a Paxton supercharger on one prototype to evaluate performance differences. Shelby had his crews fit the long, narrow sequential turn signals taken from the 1965 Thunderbird onto another prototype. He liked both of these ideas and planned to use them in coming years.

Early in the year, Ford pulled the GT40 program away from Holman Moody, and all the Mk IIs arrived at Shelby's shops with the assignment to prepare them for Daytona, Sebring, and Le Mans. One of the mechanics, Bernie Kretzschmar, who prepared GT350Rs for competition, recalled the transition: "One day the guys came in and opened the nearest door and pushed all of the Mustangs outside, covered them up with car covers, and brought in the new Ford GT Mark IIs through the other door. Those new GTs made the Daytona Coupes look like dinosaurs. And Carroll couldn't give them away. He came down into the shop and offered them to any of us who wanted one for only five grand, and there were no takers."

The already-raced Daytona coupes with advertised prices around $8,700 languished while mechanics prepared the GTs. At Daytona with Ken Miles and Lloyd Ruby co-driving, one of the cars, GT103, finished first. At Sebring, Miles and Bruce McLaren came in second in the same car. Shelby appeared to be off to a good start, but Le Mans is seldom an easy race for newcomers and Ferrari always is an unrelenting competitor.

Shelby's dealers, who were also Ford dealers, began receiving comments from buyers and those who decided not to purchase the car. Some complained that the GT350s had only two seats. Others wanted colors that were different from Wimbledon White with blue stripes. Owners disliked the loud exhaust, the loud differential, and the hard suspension. Customers who hadn't purchased a car said they wanted an automatic transmission. Some commented that

In a converted hanger at Los Angeles International Airport, Shelby converted the streetable 1965 GT350 into the track-only GT350R. While only 37 were built, it dominated B Production. *David Friedman collection*

the car didn't look distinctive enough to merit the price difference. They all seemed to want a Shelby Mustang that was more Mustang and less Shelby. Carroll's car was rough, raucous, and rowdy. Shelby, Miles, and Remington had not compromised on the car, and they could do it that way only because Ford's Total Performance program not only permitted it, but Lee Iacocca *insisted* on it.

Most magazine editors, on the other hand, marveled at the car. Here was something American, available fully equipped (such as it was) for about $4,500 that steered by turning the wheel or pressing the right foot! Shelby quoted performance figures that no magazine ever dreamed of: 0–60 miles per hour in 5.7 seconds, with a top speed of 133 miles per hour. While none of the magazines had Ken Miles to accelerate for them, they loved Carroll Shelby and accepted the car—for the most part.

Following Jerry Titus's story in March, *Sports Car Graphic* took another look at the car in late summer. An editor commented that the noise level inside the car "felt as though the [exhaust] pipes came in at each window and plugged in, stethoscope-style, at each ear." Steve Smith in *Car and Driver* magazine's May 1965 road test report had perhaps the most eloquent and backhanded compliment when he called the 1965 GT350 "a brand-new, clapped-out race car."

Shelby had initially mounted the spare wheel inside the passenger compartment and fit the battery into the trunk. Each change provided better balance, but customers disliked having battery fumes seep into the interior as well as the scant luggage space. After completing the initial 100 cars, Shelby relocated the battery to the engine compartment. The large tire would have to wait until the next model year. Neither California nor New Jersey permitted exhausts ahead of the rear tires. Some owners forwarded to Shelby tickets they received for illegally loud or improperly placed exhaust systems. The Detroit Locker limited-slip differential was perfect for racing applications but too severe for civilians on the road. In tight maneuvering, it released traction with an unsettling bang. Owners heard the noise and feared they had broken something big and costly. The traction-bar rear suspension also was noisy and its actions abrupt.

The year 1965 was one that taught Carroll Shelby a great deal about Ford Motor Company and a lot about Mustang buyers: The customers believed they wanted a race car until they owned one. Then they realized that they wanted a quiet, comfortable car that looked like a racer. The company wanted a race car that won. Carroll Shelby quickly caught up to both concepts.

CHAPTER THREE

BUY ONE OR RENT ONE: 1966

Above: Starting in 1966, GT350s used a gas cap with the Shelby logo. A wire lanyard kept the cap from being left at a gas station.

Right: Shelby installed Plexiglas in the 1966 GT350's C-pillar to reduce the blind spot that plagued the prior year's model. Ten-spoke 14-inch aluminum wheels were optional in 1966.

Above left: **To hold down costs, Shelby installed the tachometer on the 1966 GT350 as a stand-alone unit on top of the dashboard. This mounting system also eased installation.**

Above right: **For 1966, all GT350s had exhaust pipes running all the way to the rear of the car, exiting fumes underneath the rear-bumper valance. The normal abrupt operation of the Detroit Locker differential put some buyers ill at ease, so for 1966, it was made a dealer-installed option.**

Right: **Functional scoops in front of the rear wheels directed cooling air to the rear brakes. Lessons learned on the track were applied to the road cars.**

FOR SHELBY AMERICAN'S MUSTANG OPERATIONS, 1966 WAS THE YEAR OF MEASURED RETREAT AND CALCULATED ADVANCES. The new year began early, arriving in September 1965. Ford's San Jose factory prepared for the model year changeover, a shut-down process that often took much of July and August. To be certain the plant had Shelby's requirements covered, it shipped a load of 252 final-production 1965 models to Shelby American's new Los Angeles airport facility. Changes planned for the GT350s originated from a number of sources that stretched from coast to coast, with many influences in between. Shelby and his crew had their work cut out for them as each of these changes swerved the car away from its racing origins.

California and New Jersey laws prohibited exhausts from coming out anywhere ahead of the rear wheels, so midway through 1965, Phil Remington and his mechanics fabricated special systems for these two states. By model-year end, Shelby concluded it was not worth offering—and paying for—two separate versions, so for 1966 all exhausts ran to the rear of the cars.

Remington replaced the noisy Detroit Locker rear differentials with less-expensive and more compliant Ford No-Spin units; these no longer came standard on the cars but were dealer-installed options. With the battery back in the engine compartment, the next step to making useful

Above: The front-end treatment on the 1966 GT350 was identical to the year before, except that the 1966 Mustang's grille was used, sans center-mounted galloping horse.

Above left: **For 1966, the full-length stripes were adhesive appliqués made by 3M. The stripes had been painted on in 1965. Going to tape saved time and money.** *Above right:* **Approximately one-third of the way through production of the 1966 GT350, the last of the over-ride traction bars were installed. At that point, Traction Master under-ride bars were used. This eliminated the need to cut holes in the floor, saving time and quieting the interior.**

storage space meant moving the spare wheel and tire back to the trunk. Shelby stepped down to 14-inch tires from 15s on the 1965 cars. To make this appealing, he introduced optional 14x6.5 cast-alloy wheels that weighed less than the 15-inch steels. These handsome ten-spoke models were a $267 option in 1966. For those who preferred the 15-inch size, Shelby offered a two-piece five-spoke aluminum wheel that's almost impossible for restorers to find today.

Another noisemaker went the way of civility as well. Ken Miles' override rear traction bars lingered through the 1965 carryover cars from San Jose (as did the modified front suspensions). After those 252 cars were gone, and for the remainder of the 1966s, front suspensions rode at factory settings and smaller under-ride-style traction bars appeared. These new under-mounted bars did not require the time-consuming and costly process of cutting the floorpan, inserting the bars, and mounting them inside the car. With the smaller wheels, the spare mounted in the trunk, and no more suspension pieces intruding into the passenger compartment, Ford's standard Mustang

flip-up rear seat fit into the interior. While San Jose had charged Shelby a nominal fee to delete it during assembly, now he made it a mandatory extra-price option, and back seats began appearing regularly after they had completed about 80 of the 1966 models. (Dealers also offered the seat as an option they installed.)

Other interior changes were equally cost driven. Shelby's wood steering wheel reverted to the stock Mustang GT piece. This was plastic but toned and embossed to look and feel like wood. Shelby offered an optional wood wheel, though it was different from the previous version. Peter Brock's oil pressure and tachometer pod disappeared as well. Ford incorporated an oil gauge on its 1966 instrument panel so GT350s got a free-standing "Cobra" 9,000-rpm tachometer mounted on top of the dashboard.

One change customers really welcomed was Peter Brock's rear quarter windows. These fixed-in-place Plexiglas triangles replaced the roof side panels where production cars still had vent louvers. Shelby made these available at his parts counter, and a number of 1965 cars

Due to Ford's production schedule, Shelby had to use 252 1965 GT350s for 1966. They were converted at his plant at Los Angeles International Airport and were considered carryover cars, which still used the modified suspension of the 1965 cars.

Left: When John Hertz started his automobile rental business in 1925, he painted his cars black with gold stripes. Shelby and his general manager, Peyton Cramer, did their homework when they made their sales presentation to Hertz executives in 1965, flying a GT350 to New York City, painted in the company colors. They got the contract.

Below: It was no surprise that GT350s and GT350Hs used Goodyear tires; Shelby was the Goodyear racing-tire distributor for 11 western states. The dual bronze metallic stripes went all the way to the bottom of both front and rear valances.

GT350Hs came with a back seat and a radio for customer comfort. Shelby's contract called for the vehicles to use an automatic transmission, but approximately 100 used 4-speed manual transmissions.

and several non-Shelby Mustangs received the conversion. Purists bemoaned the option, but the addition of a no-additional-charge automatic—Ford's beefy three-speed C-4—made the car attractive to a broader audience. GT350s equipped with either the four-speed manual or three-speed automatic sold for $4,428, a $119 price reduction from $4,527 in 1965. And if that wasn't good enough, Ford offered many of the colors in its paint palette for Shelby's Mustangs. As well as Wimbledon White, buyers could now order Guardsman Blue, Candy Apple Red, Sapphire Blue, Ivy Green, and Raven Black. The availability of black brought Shelby his biggest single customer for any of his products.

Early in Shelby's relationship with Ford Motor Company, Ray Geddes introduced Carroll to Peyton Cramer, who worked in Ford's comptroller's office in Dearborn. Geddes hoped to entice Cramer to transfer to Shelby American as general manager. After a year of commuting between Dearborn and Venice, Cramer moved his family to California in mid-1963 to assume the position full time. In 1964, Cramer helped Shelby establish High Performance Motors. Shelby planned to sell Cobras, the Sunbeam Tiger he had also developed for Ford, and Mustangs. Ford balked at that part of the plan, since its own dealers carried the Shelby Mustang as a traffic draw, even if they sold very few.

As the GT350 program had geared up, Shelby and Cramer recognized the need for a lot more factory space. Cramer located two vacant hangars that belonged to North American Aviation on Imperial Highway along the east edge of Los Angeles International Airport. Because the airport owned the land, and North American had constructed the buildings, the best Cramer could accomplish was a month-to-month lease. Neither he nor Shelby let on

to corporate how temporary and tenuous their hold was on that fundamental part of the business.

In mid-1965, Cramer left the general manager position and took over sales for Shelby American. Shelby had heard in early 1965 that Hertz Rent-a-Car Corporation, based in New York City, had established a program for executive and business travelers with good credit and clean driving records. America's number-two car rental agency, Avis, dogged Hertz for the number-one position in car rentals, and during this period both companies initiated distinctive marketing programs specifically aimed at the growing number of business travelers. In about a dozen major U.S. cities, qualified drivers who were members of the Hertz Sports Car Club could rent Corvettes. In late October, Shelby asked Cramer to see if Hertz might be interested in buying a couple dozen GT350s for their club.

"I went to the library first," Cramer recalled, "just to do some research. I found that back in 1925 when they started, John Hertz, the founder, had acquired an existing livery service that used to make its own cars in Chicago." Hertz's plan back then was to rent self-drive cars to potential customers as a means of encouraging sales. To identify the livery service and promote his self-drive idea, Hertz painted all his cars black and gold, one of his favorite color combinations.

Above left: **Not every GT350H wore full-length stripes down the hood, roof, and trunk. But they all used rocker-panel stripes to identify themselves. Stylist Peter Brock originally penned the rocker stripes for the 1965 GT350, and they became indelibly linked to the Shelby Mustang.** *Above right:* **Because the 1966 GT350H used competition metallic pads and linings, many customers complained that the brakes were inadequate. Until they warmed up, they were about as effective as opening a door and dragging a foot. This placard on the dashboard warned drivers about the brakes' behavior.**

"When I went to New York," Cramer told Wallace Wyss in his book *Shelby's Wildlife*, "I had prepared a black-and-gold prototype GT350 and I had it flown to New York. When I met with their executives, they were impressed. I proposed offering a special-model Shelby, painted in their traditional colors." Hertz executives suggested adding the "H" to the rocker panel tape logo, and calling it the GT350H. On November 23, 1965, they placed an order with Cramer for 200 cars. Depending on customer response, Hertz also hinted that they might increase the order.

Hertz immediately launched a promotional blitz alerting customers that it offered GT350s at various airport locations. With the ad campaign underway, reservations coming in, and club membership swelling, Hertz ordered an additional 800 cars the very next month, on December 21.

Hertz wanted all 1,000 cars to have automatic transmissions and radios. But specifications got confused during production. Shelby delivered the first 85 cars with four-speed manuals. Shelby American did ship the first 200

in black with gold stripes as Cramer's prototype had been. However, because Hertz had assumed—but had not specified—its color scheme on the larger second order, the next batch of 230 cars went out in red, blue, white, and green, all with gold stripes. At that point, Hertz clarified its desires. Cramer's paint scheme had captivated them. The remaining 570 cars were black with gold stripes. All interiors were black. The rear seats used factory-standard narrow seatbelts, although Shelby's SCCA-approved wide belts remained up front. Depending on location, Hertz rented the cars for between $13 and $17 per day, or $54 to $70 for a week. Due to geography and other considerations, mileage charges varied from $0.13 to $0.17 per mile as well. One constant was the age requirement. Hertz only offered the cars to drivers who were older than 25.

Shelby's Mustangs have been surrounded as much by myth as fact since they first appeared. One of the great mysteries concerned racers who, legend had it, rented Shelby GT350H models to drive to the races and then drove the cars *in the races* while they were there. While

Above left: **Ever the master promoter, Shelby was never one to overlook a high-visibility location for his logo, as evidenced by the center cap on the wheel of a 1966 GT350.** *Above right:* **The interior of the 1966 GT350H was standard Shelby, including the 3-inch lap belts. The circular emblem on the brake pedal indicates that this particular vehicle has the troublesome competition brakes.**

the Hertz cars had standard Shelby brakes with their sintered metallic linings that worked best when warm, the cars had no roll bars. But that didn't deter at least two determined drivers.

Retired California racer Jim Gessner and his buddy, the late John Lifield, became regulars at a Hertz airport counter outside Baltimore, Maryland. "For three months in the summer of 1966," Gessner recalled with a laugh, "I picked up that black-and-gold manual-transmission car, drove it to the storage warehouse where John and I kept our spare wheels. We had a full set mounted with Goodyear racing blue dots. We'd bolt in the roll cage and head over to Marlboro Raceway in Marlboro." By August, rental counter personnel in Baltimore were suspicious enough to deny him a car. As the season wound to a close and Hertz caught on to what they and other racers were doing, Gessner and Lifield ventured farther and farther out of town to rent cars for their final races.

For 1966, Shelby withdrew his own Mustang team from racing. The factory effort had provided the anticipated

promotional value but the Ford division now needed Shelby's help on the so-far-unsuccessful GT40 racing program. Shelby initiated incentive payments to his privateers. Each time a GT350 won, its owner received a $150 check from Shelby American, and second-place finishes earned the owner $75. Shelby American completed the remaining 1965 R-model Mustangs during 1966, 20 in all, five of which they shipped to Australia to compete in the Tasman Series for production models. Each car received the 1966-style front grille as mechanics assembled the racers in late 1965.

In addition to the 1,000 Hertz cars, Shelby American produced 1,370 regular fastbacks throughout 1966 model year. They turned out four more drag race cars as well. On top of these were two other limited-production runs.

During the summer of 1965, Shelby had experimented with mounting a Paxton supercharger on one of his cars. By late spring 1966, he was ready to send a prototype out for magazine testing to gain feedback on its viability as a new product. In July 1966, *Car Life* magazine, published in

Newport Beach, California, about 30 miles down I-405 from Shelby's facilities at the L.A. airport, got its hands on one of the first GT350S prototypes. This was an innovative blend that mounted Paxton's centrifugal supercharger atop an otherwise "stock" Shelby GT350. Magazine editor Dennis Shattuck and editorial director Dean Batchelor got an unusual car to evaluate, one that pushed the envelope in still another direction: This car used the C-4 automatic transmission.

"Combining three such unlikely elements as a highly-tuned and modified Mustang, a centrifugal-type supercharger, and an automatic transmission is at best a chancy project," the writer opened his story. "Any two of these elements would seem at the outset virtually incompatible. . . .

"The outcome is a docile, four-seat sports car that will out-thrust any 400-plus cubic-inch sedan on pure acceleration, or thrash it into submission on crooked roads. And, for only 289 cubic inches of displacement, this must be regarded as at least mildly sensational." The magazine story's technical analysis explained how this combination functioned.

By gutting the interior, removing the rear bumper, replacing the steel front bumper with a fiberglass piece, and installing a Plexiglas rear window, Shelby kept the weight of the 1965 GT350R down, helping it to trounce the competition in events like the Road America 500 of September, 1965, shown here. *David Friedman collection*

"The automatic transmission smoothes out the highly-tuned engine's inherent lumpy low-speed characteristics with pleasant part-throttle operation. . . . Where the engine needs its biggest help is at the very low end of its operation scale—below 2,000 rpm. Here the torque converter effectively multiplies what power there is into a useful quantity. The supercharger at idling speed does not achieve an effective boost so the converter gives it breathing space by letting the engine turn up more rpm than would direct gearing. Where the converter phases out, the supercharger begins to pump—and the engine really starts to climb the power curve."

The 1966 GT350H was no different under the hood from regular GT350s. That means a 306-horsepower, 289-cubic-inch V-8, which was ideal for fulfilling Walter Mitty dreams. Sixty miles per hour only needed 6.6 seconds to attain.

Shelby supplied Hertz with a total vehicle run in 1966 of 1,000 vehicles, of which 825 were painted black and bronze. All it took to rent one was to be older than 25.

Despite this, performance statistics didn't quicken the editors' pulses, nor did it create long lines at Shelby's front door. The standard GT350 accelerated from 0–60 miles per hour in 6.8 seconds. With the supercharger, the time dropped 0.6 seconds, to 6.2. The standing-start quarter-mile happened in 14.7 seconds at 90 miles per hour with the standard GT350, and 14.0 seconds at 92 miles per hour. The supercharger option added $600 to the price. Despite the initial "mildly sensational" characterization, the story steered its readers away from Shelby's version and recommended that, at $430 and direct from Paxton, they supercharge a standard-issue Mustang GT themselves, achieving Shelby performance at a lower cost.

As he had done after evaluating his first supercharged prototype, Shelby filed the idea away. Then he completed another project with so limited a production series that for years even enthusiasts deeply immersed in Shelby lore considered it just another Shelby Mustang myth. In reality, the final six 1966 models, numbers 2375 through 2380, were convertibles—three white, one red, one blue, and one green—that Shelby prepared as gifts for his wife, his secretary, himself, and three other unidentified individuals who had helped him in earlier days. Shelby used the red convertible and his wife drove the blue one for several months until Hayward Motors, north of San Jose, sold her car and the white convertibles later in 1966. Hayward

Shelby charged Hertz $3,547 for the 1966 GT350, plus $45.45 for the Shelby-installed AM radio. The 1,000 vehicles built for Hertz made up nearly 40 percent of Shelby's business in 1966, putting him firmly in the black.

While most 1966 GT359Hs were painted in black with bronze stripes, other colors were used, such as Sapphire Blue. After Hertz sold the vehicles, private owners might have installed aftermarket wheels to personalize their car.

Once the stock of over-ride traction bars had been exhausted, under-ride bars were used, hanging down from the rear axle forward to the underside of the floorpan. Like other GT350s, the Hertz model enjoyed a 52/48 front/rear weight distribution.

ultimately sold the green car as well.

While Shelby American had quit racing its own "factory" GT350R models at the end of 1965, it was far from finished with racing efforts that kept Ford's performance dealer network happy. Shelby had discontinued production of the 289 Cobra, yet the 427 still drew people into showrooms even if scarcely any sold. The GT350 Mustangs attracted a crowd, and these fed dads and husbands into station wagons or four-door sedans. But salespeople learned that these customers paid attention to racing on weekends.

Ironically, after all of Shelby's work to get GT350s qualified as B-production sports cars, the SCCA announced a National Sedan Championship for 1966, as part of the Fédération Internationale de l'Automobile (FIA) Appendix J Group 2. The production 4.7-liter, 289 cubic-inch notchback qualified for the A/Sedan class because one of the rules required cars to have four permanent seats. This automatically eliminated the GT350, which had been

homologated as a two-seater. The SCCA conceived two parallel-running series, one for amateur racers and one for professionals. The amateur class was comprised of about 50 events contested regionally that culminated in the top three finishers from the six regions competing in the American Road Race of Champions (ARRC). Professional races covered longer distances, ranging upwards from two hours and 200 miles. The professional series constituted seven races, known as the Trans-American Sedan Championship, or Trans-Am. The season-long prize for this category was a manufacturer's trophy.

Sports Car Graphic magazine editor and racer Jerry Titus had won the B-Production SCCA national title in a Shelby GT350 in 1965. Dearborn wanted an official Ford entry for the new series. As if Shelby didn't already have enough to do, he got orders from world headquarters to get involved. Like previous commands from Frey and Beebe, these came with an unspecified budget. (One of the

Not all GT350Hs lead pampered lives: Some were driven to local racetracks and flogged unmercifully, then returned to the rental counter. Hertz worked to minimize such antics, but tales abound of mechanical mayhem. *Randy Leffingwell*

A 1966 GT350 works to prevent a Cobra from taking the corner as they battle during the Monterey Historic Automobile Races at Laguna Seca. In most cases, the Cobra would pull ahead.

methods Shelby used to stay financially solvent in racing was to work on a "cost-plus" basis. Shelby acquired the parts or talents and added a percentage on top as justifiable expenses and profit to Shelby American.)

Chuck Cantwell had joined Shelby American in Venice in 1964 and he made the move to the airport in 1965. He got the assignment to direct the development of the Trans-Am race car. Shelby ordered 20 notchbacks stripped to minimum equipment and ultimately converted to virtual GT350R specifications at the airport shops. But his first efforts were much more modest.

"I think our first Trans-Am budget was five thousand dollars," Cantwell told fellow Shelby American employee Dave Friedman in his book *Remembering the Shelby Years*. "We went to a dealer, bought a car, and converted it into a racing car that would conform to the existing Trans-Am

rules. We used it as a test car . . . That car also was used to solidify the specifications for the customer cars. All of the race cars that we built for customers in 1966 scored points for Ford when they placed, and by the time it came down to the last race at Riverside, Ford had a chance to win the championship. So we pulled a customer race car we were building off the line and set it up for Jerry Titus to drive. He won the race and Ford won the championship."

Shelby's Group 2 Mustangs won points for Ford in five out of the seven professional races that year. John McComb and Pete Talbert finished third in car No. 3 at the Mid-America 300 in Wentzville, Missouri, in June, and McComb and Brad Brooker won the Pan-American Six Hour in car No. 12 on September 10 at Green Valley, Texas. At the season finale at the Riverside 4-Hour one week later on the 18th, McComb and Brooker chased race-winner Titus across the finish line of a very dramatic race, coming in fourth place again in car No. 12.

By late September, Carroll Shelby's long year was nearly over. Twelve months earlier, in late September 1965, Henry Ford II had called him, Don Frey, Leo Beebe, and Ray Geddes into his office. That June, for the second year in a row, Ferraris had humiliated Ford GT40s at Le Mans in 1965. When the four visitors entered Ford's office, the chairman was wearing a lapel pin and he pointed to several more on his desk. The pin said, "Ford Wins Le Mans 1966." As they picked them up, Shelby recalled that Ford said "Don't make me a liar." They talked briefly and Ford dismissed them. As they reached the door, Don Frey turned.

"How much money can I spend?" Frey asked. The question was pertinent: Ford had just spent $1.7 million and lost. Ford said, "I never said anything about money," and the message was clear.

For 1965, Ford had pushed Shelby to get a bigger hammer and it spread responsibility among other Le Mans entrants. Shelby American had entered two cars with 427-cubic-inch engines. Ford Advanced Vehicles had one with the 4.7 liter. Scuderia Filipinetti, the Geneva-based Swiss national team, and Rob Walker, a retired racer and descendant of the Johnny Walker distillers of Great Britain, each ran a car with a 5.3-liter engine, while Ford of France competed with a GT40 roadster powered by the 4.7-liter. One Shelby car crashed and all the others broke engines or gearboxes. The best Ford finish, again, was a car owned by Charles and William Hurlock of A.C. Cars Ltd., who had

Above left: Group 2 Mustangs were prepared by Shelby to GT350R specs, with the exception of window glass and a full interior. In this car's second race at Green Valley, Texas, John McComb won the six-hour Trans-Am race by six laps. *Above right:* Driver John McComb got the 1966 Shelby Trans-Am race car in September 1966, and went on to win his first race with the car at the Continental Divide SCCA national at Castle Rock, Colorado. *Facing page:* This 1966 Group 2 coupe was built for Shelby driver Ken Miles to compete with in the growing Trans Am series, but before he had a chance to drive it, he was killed at Riverside Raceway on August 17, 1966, testing a GT40 car prototype

Above: As the Group 2 race cars used a Mustang GT as their starting point, the grille was home to fog lamps. High-intensity driving lights were fitted to the fog-lamp housings to provide better illumination during night driving at some of the Trans-Am races.

Below: Covered lights kept glass on the racetrack to a minimum during a wreck. Removal of the front bumper helped balance the front/rear weight distribution, as well as lighten the vehicle. Behind the grille was an 18-quart Ford Galaxie radiator.

Below: **Trans-Am regulations required that Group 2 cars have a full interior and be capable of seating four occupants. A full roll cage was installed.**

entered one of Shelby's Cobra coupes. They came in eighth behind five Ferraris and two Porsches. Soon after their meeting with Henry Ford II, and with the vaguely defined "000" account seemingly infinitely funded, Frey authorized construction of a full chassis dynamometer. Ford engineers ran GT40s for 24 hours at a time to simulate race loads on complete power trains.

When Ford returned to France in 1966, it invaded Le Mans like a juggernaut. Thirteen of 55 starters were GT40s. When the checkered flag fell at 4 p.m. on Sunday, June 19, Shelby-prepared GT40 Mk IIs had finished first, second, and third in a near-squadron-like assault on the finish line. The slowest of the trio outran the nearest Ferrari,

All 16 Group 2 1966 Mustangs were essentially R-model Shelbys under the hood, as the Shelby American racing 289-cubic-inch engine was topped by an aluminum high-rise manifold and a 715-cubic-feet-per-minute Holley. Output was in the region of 350 horsepower.

The 34-gallon fuel tank was constructed using two regular Mustang gas tanks, cutting them, and welding them together. The 3 1/2-inch quick-release cap and splash funnel are pure R-model.

finishing in eighth place, by 469 kilometers (293 miles); the fastest Ford was another hundred miles behind that. Experienced race-car manufacturers Eric Broadley, John Cooper, and Colin Chapman each had tried to tell Ford it required a minimum of three years of hard work to develop a Le Mans-winning race car. When Ford won, no one chanted "I told you so." Instead, racers and race-car makers everywhere marveled at how well they had done it in only three years.

Victory is addictive. Decisive victories are especially enthralling. For Henry Ford II, it was vital that the world of motor racing know that 1966 was no fluke. Shelby had been an indispensable element in defeating Enzo Ferrari,

but years later he acknowledged that, "Henry Ford won Le Mans single-handedly." There were no new lapel pins in September decreeing Ford Wins Again in 1967. The four men who held the precious originals knew they needed no further coaxing or threatening. If Shelby was stretched thin, orders from world headquarters would reduce Shelby's distractions.

One of the first distractions to disappear was 427 Cobra production. Dealers could no longer sell them, racers no longer wanted them, and their cult status had not yet mushroomed, so assembly essentially stopped in late November 1966. In a decision he later regretted but which helped his financial situation at the time, Shelby agreed to

This 1966 Shelby convertible was the third of six built, serial No. 2377. Note the lack of Le Mans stripes. *Right:* Shelby's 1966 convertible was standard GT350 with the exception of the air conditioning. The dash-mounted tachometer was labeled Cobra, lest a driver forget what car he was in. *Above right:* Shelby used a simple system to identify his vehicles on the ID plate. The number 6 stands for a 1966 car, the S means a street vehicle, and the last four numbers are the build number.

Six Shelby convertibles were built in 1966, not originally intended for sale to the public. Instead, they were gifts to select Shelby employees. Shelby kept this red convertible for his own use.

It's not a mirage; this is a genuine 1966 Shelby convertible. Functional brake cooling scoops debuted in 1966. The 14-inch chromed Magnum 500s were not available on regular GT350s.

The mounting holes for the original Mustang galloping horse are visible in the center of the grille. Shelby utilized the stock Mustang grille, but mounted the fender emblem.

An air-conditioning compressor is not a normal sight in the engine compartment of a 1966 GT350, but this convertible was Carroll Shelby's personal car, and what Carroll wants, Carroll gets.

Carroll Shelby's personal 1966 GT350 used Traction Master under-rider traction bars to control axle hop under heavy acceleration. Heavily optioned, it was one of six ragtops ever built.

Far left: Candy Apple Red was a Shelby color in 1966, and Shelby had his personal GT350 convertible painted in the head-turning hue.

Left: Clean and proportionally ideal, the 1966 Shelby GT350 had a full slate of Shelby enhancements, including rear-brake cooling scoops, under-rider traction bars, and five-spoke chromed Magnum wheels.

In its element, this GT40 Mk. IV fights for control as it comes through turn four at Laguna Seca Raceway.

sell the name "Cobra" to Ford. Eight more cars appeared with either 289- or 427-cubic-inch engines in 1967; the airport facility assembled another 11 in 1968, and the "final" Cobra, CSX 6125, left Shelby for England on February 24, 1969.

Shelby had new personnel from Dearborn to help expand production of the new-bodied 1967 model. Ford had set its target at 4,000 units. And Henry Ford II had set his sights on victory number two.

Above: Stock 15-inch wheels were surrounded by Casler "cheater slicks" in 1966, and the exhaust was routed out in front of the rear wheels, similar to 1965 GT350s. *Right:* With the exception of a roll bar, this 1966 Shelby drag car's interior was standard Shelby, which is to say, standard Mustang. Unlike the 1965 GT350R, this vehicle was not stripped of its interior, although a Hurst Competition-Plus shifter was installed.

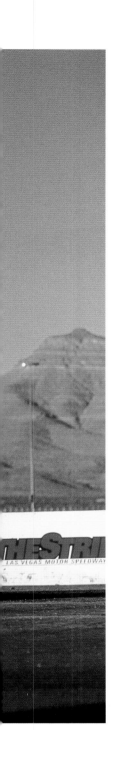

Above top: **Shelby built nine drag cars in 1965 and four in 1966, including this example, No. 6S011. It's interesting to see the bumpers are still on the vehicle.** *Above bottom:* **The 289-cubic-inch engine fed power through a 4.86:1 gear set. Koni rear shocks minimized axle hop. Cure-Ride 90/10 up-lock front shocks maximized weight transfer for traction. They were stiffer than stock shocks, but not as hard as racing shocks.**

Left: **In its element, a factory 1966 Shelby drag car lunges for the finish light. Factory-installed equipment included a scattershield, a driveshaft safety loop, and AFX rear traction bars.**

Below: **The tall hood scoop was designed to ingest large quantities of cool air and ram it into the Holley carburetor.**

Above: **The quarter-mile flashes past as a 1966 Shelby GT350 factory drag-car driver rows through the gears. Gus Zuidema of Lebanon Valley, New York, covered the quarter-mile in 12.68 seconds in a factory drag car.**

Right: Under the lift-off hood, the engine was stock Shelby, which meant a 306-horsepower 289-cubic-inch Ford V-8. A heater/defroster delete option was offered in '66.

Above: Externally, the Shelby factory drag car looked like a stock 1966 GT350, but a wealth of improvements under the skin allowed the vehicles to be highly competitive. Belanger drag headers were designed for this brutal environment.

CHAPTER FOUR

STYLING BREAKS RULES AND ENGINES GET BIGGER: 1967

Right: Ford took the checkered flag at the 1967 Le Mans again with this Mk IV GT40, chassis J6, driven by Dan Gurney and A. J. Foyt. Entered by Shelby American, it incorporated a bulge in the driver's door to clear Gurney's helmet. A rules change for 1967 allowed a narrow windshield to be used. The designers narrowed the cockpit, reducing the frontal area and its subsequent drag.

Below: Mk IV GT40s were built using bonded-aluminum honeycomb panels. Racing weight was 2,650 pounds, and the 500-horsepower 427-cubic-inch engine could propel the vehicle to 230 miles per hour.

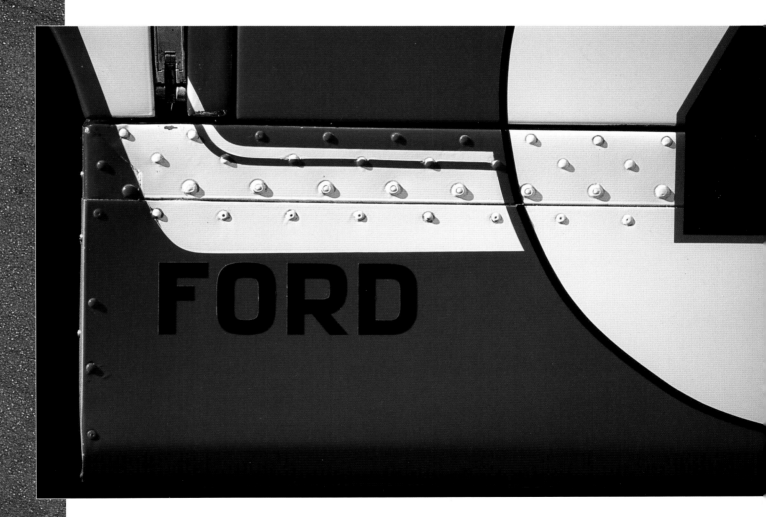

Above: **In order to increase downforce on the front tires, the Mk IV GT40 used a dropped nose, as seen on chassis J11. Slab sides and a lengthened tail improved aerodynamics and high-speed stability.**

NO ONE WHO WAS INVOLVED WITH FORD'S RACING ACCOMPLISHMENTS WOULD THINK OTHERWISE: 1966 HAD BEEN A LONG YEAR. For Fred Goodell, the pace was almost relentless. He never imagined how much more frantic it could get.

Ray Geddes and Jacque Passino had singled out Goodell. His accomplishments and his personality made him their top candidate to be chief engineer at Shelby American. Goodell was working as the chief engineer in Ford's international division. He was not seeking another job or a transfer to milder climates. But Geddes and Passino worked for Don Frey who, as Ford division general manager by then, didn't have to take no for an answer. Goodell found excuses to delay and postpone the inevitable, but by mid-year 1966 he had visited Shelby American, seen the challenges there, and decided to accept the job. Along with Fred Goodell, Dearborn had loaned Shelby the services of stylist Chuck McHose.

John Kerr had taken over for Peyton Cramer as Shelby American general manager and he was glad to have another Ford insider on site. Whether this was for commiseration or for production is still up for debate. As Goodell told Dave Friedman, "I became Carroll's chief engineer, and after about a week on the job, I said, 'Holy shit—this is a mess.'"

Ford's planners had expanded Shelby Mustang production to 4,000 units for 1967. When Goodell arrived

Six of the Mk IV GT40s gathered at the 2003 Monterey Historic Automobile Races at Laguna Seca to honor Ford's history of Motorsports. Red No. 1 in the foreground was entered by Shelby American and went on to win the 1967 24 Hours of Le Mans.

three months into the production year, mechanics in the hangars had completed just 40 cars. More than a year earlier, Shelby American had received photographs, dimensions, and scale drawings of the new 1967 model. Producing thousands of cars, Shelby had learned, was big business. It frequently amounted to meeting urgent deadlines that stole him away from the problem solving that gave him pleasure—making racing cars go faster. Based on Sperlich's best estimates of what General Motors, Chrysler, and American Motors had on test tracks for 1967 and 1968, Ford's engine division had offered Shelby the big-block 428 Police Interceptor engine. Hal Sperlich, Don Frey's deputy in product planning and the actual driving

force behind the Mustang's development, had suggested to Shelby that instead of racing engines and suspensions, Carroll put his effort and investment on the outside of his Mustangs rather than beneath the hood, under the car body, or inside the wheel wells. Shelby had been his own boss through 1965; he didn't argue now. Following the intuition that yielded the GT350 designation, Shelby named the Interceptor car the GT500.

Dearborn stylist Chuck McHose shared with Peter Brock the assignment to give the next generation Shelbys their own distinctive appearance. They received a pre-production 1967 model to work from. Together with Pete Stacey, whom Shelby had hired to assist Brock, the

Below right: A smattering of Shelby enhancements were sprinkled around an essentially stock 1967 Mustang interior in the GT350S. A beefy Hurst shifter was bolted to a four-speed transmission. *Upper right:* It cost $549.00 to have the letter "S" placed on the rocker panel of a 1967 GT350. The value was under the hood, where a Paxton supercharger was installed, boosting horsepower to 390. It helped bring the 0–60 mile-per-hour time from 7.1 seconds to 6.2 for a regular GT350.

three men styled the differences that made the GT350 and the GT500 look wilder than regular production fastbacks. They lengthened the hood 3 inches and recessed the grille deeper into the front cavity, closer to the radiator. They made master drawings from the technical blueprints Ford had sent, but later confirmed and adjusted dimensions on the actual car. Pete Stacey suggested using four-beam headlight configurations to differentiate their car from regular production models, and he proposed mounting the high beams together in the center of the grille.

The 1965 and 1966 models had used a hood scoop. Brock's early prototypes set the air intake at the rear of the scoop to take advantage of the low-air-pressure area at

the base of the windshield. But he and Shelby felt the car looked more balanced with the opening facing forward and mounted farther down the hood. For 1967, McHose and Brock integrated the scoop into the fiberglass hood so it appeared to be integral to the design rather than an add-on part. They added side air scoops resembling the GT40's rear brake-cooling ears onto the sides of the roof behind the doors where Brock had installed Plexiglas windows in 1966. The designers took another visual cue from the GT40 and the Cobras before it. Racing mechanics mounted side marker lights to illuminate the numbers at night, making it easier for Ford timers and race officials to count laps and distinguish one car from another. Brock and McHose put red

bullet lights just inside the trailing edges of the roof scoops.

Aside from the center-mounted headlights, the Shelby Mustang's next most notable feature is its large rear spoiler. Ford designers had extended the 1967 roofline out from the middle of the rear deck lid to the end of the body. This was similar to, and— according to Ford studio chief Joe Oros— was somewhat inspired by, the tail that Brock conceived for the Cobra coupes. To that rear end, Brock had added a large, nearly vertical air spoiler that he and Alex "Skeet" Kerr had devised. Brock and Kerr adapted their rear spoiler and set it over the Mustang taillight valence. Sequential taillights taken from the Ford Thunderbird and Mercury Cougar that Shelby had tested on the earlier prototype now went onto the production 1967. Everything conspired to add a strong visual identity to the 1967 Shelby Mustangs.

Shelby's ever-growing engineering staff, aided and abetted by recent Dearborn emigrants, reworked the Mustang suspension to soften the ride. Dealers made it clear that buyers who had always wanted a race car became far less certain once they drove their 1965 street GT350s off the lot. Much of that harshness disappeared when the 1966 models reverted to stock front-suspension mount points, and the 2-inch-wider track of the new cars seemed to soften the ride even further. In addition, Shelby's crew modestly resized the front anti-sway bar, down to 0.94-inch diameter from 1.0 in the previous generation. They retained the variable-rate springs that Phil Remington

and Ken Miles had created for the early cars. Some of the suspension modifications also reduced production costs. For example, engineers replaced the expensive Dutch-import Koni adjustable shock absorbers with U.S.-made Gabriel adjustable units.

Shelby carried over the same solid valve-lifter 289-cubic-inch 306-horsepower engine he had used in the 1965 and 1966 models. He used the cast-aluminum high-rise intake manifold and Holley four-barrel carburetor, but

Airflow to the radiator suffered when the high-beam headlights were mounted in the center of the grille. This rare 1967 GT350S generated plenty of heat as it kicked out 390 horsepower. The large chrome circular container in the foreground is the air-cleaner housing.

high-horsepower cars in the hands of drivers with limited experience. For Shelby's street adaptation, he fitted the 428 with two Holley 650-cubic-foot-per-minute four-barrel carburetors mounted on a medium-rise intake manifold. Hydraulic lifters quieted engine noise for the customers who still believed they wanted a race car but knew they didn't want the noise or harshness of a real race car. To that end, engineers deleted the "Monte Carlo bar" that tied the shock absorber tower to the firewall, though they kept the fender-to-fender "export brace."

One big problem with the 1967 Mustang, whether Shelby's or Ford's, was that it was bigger. The car had grown not only in dimensions but also in weight. Lee Iacocca's original 2,500-pound coupe had swollen to about 2,800 pounds in Shelby's 1966 GT350. Weight surged to 3,286 pounds in the 428-engined GT500. While the engine's additional 49 horsepower nearly compensated for 500 pounds of extra weight, nothing could help the weight bias that this heavier engine brought to the front. The GT500 balanced out at 57 percent on the front tires, 43 percent on the rears. The new GT350, whose engine weighed 176 pounds less, was better at 53 front, 47 rear. Fuel economy, something very few people considered in 1967 when gasoline sold for $0.33 per gallon, was another gripe that piled up against the GT500. The 8-barrel Cobra Jet was good for 6 to 11 miles per gallon, depending on who drove it and how vigorously. *Sports Car Graphic* averaged 9.4 miles per gallon during its test.

Car and Driver magazine placed the new GT500 in the context of 1965 and 1966 GT350s when it tested the new car for its February 1967 issue. "The '65 GT350 was a hot-rodder's idea of a sports car," its editor wrote. He continued, calling the early car "a rough-riding bronco that was as exciting to drive as a Maserati 300S, and about as marketable a proposition. The traction bars clanked, the side exhausts were deafening, the clutch was better than an advanced Charles Atlas program, and when the ratcheting-type limited-slip differential unlocked, it sounded like the

federal emissions standards denied him further use of the steel-tube exhaust headers. Ford had rated the 428 police car engine at 335 horsepower with its standard cam. (This same cam would see service in the 428 Cobra Jet engines in GT500KR models in 1968.) The extremely conservative figure solved two problems: It helped Ford's efforts to sneak the engine into a lower class in NHRA drag racing while it also helped deflect concern over performance versus safety—from an insurance industry growing wary of

At the 1967 24 Hours of Le Mans race, Team Claude Dubois entered a 1965 GT350R, serial #5R539. It finished 58 laps before being sidelined with a broken transmission neck. Note the special windshield wiper, designed to clear the glass on the high-speed Mulsanne Straight. *David Friedman collection*

A roll bar was included as part of the basic 1967 GT350 package, but the shoulder harness was a $50.76 option.

rear axle had cracked in half. It rode like a Conestoga wagon and steered like a 1936 REO coal truck—and we loved it.

"We drove, briefly, a '67 GT350 and noted how busy and mechanical the engine sounds. Jumping into the GT500," the unidentified writer continued, "the most marked difference was in engine noise, which is practically non-existent in the 428-engined car except for a motor-boating throb. . . . All the viciousness had gone out of the car, without any lessening of its animal vitality. It still reacts positively, but to a much lighter touch.

"That then is the GT500, a grown-up sports car for smooth touring. No more wham-bam, thank-you-ma'am, just a purring, well-controlled tiger. Like Shelby says, 'This is the first car I'm really proud of.'

"Right. We've come a long way since bib overalls, too, Shel."

Car and Driver, which tested cars with a driver only, minimal equipment, and hard launches, achieved 0–60 miles-per-hour times of 6.5 seconds. But *Road & Track,* running its evaluations with a driver and test equipment operator, had a gentler hand on the controls and could do no better than 7.2. Somewhat later in the production run, Shelby offered the 427-cubic-inch side-oiler engine as an option, but Shelby American manufactured fewer than 50 examples.

While Shelby diminished and decreased some of the race-car characteristics from the new cars, he shrewdly installed features that restored the *sensation* of race cars.

Fiberglass was the material of choice for the hood, which incorporated an integral functional scoop. On the GT350S, it just fed air into the engine compartment for cooling. The lower side scoops fed cooling air to the rear drum brakes.

A bigger hammer was introduced in 1967 with the release of the GT500. With a big-block in the Mustang inventory, Shelby took advantage to increase power with more cubic inches. The huge headers are owner-installed.

Shelby welded a roll bar to the floor pan in the fastbacks and attached to it a pair of inertia-reel-fed shoulder harnesses that supplemented Ford's standard lap belt. Federal safety regulations required over-the-shoulder across-the-chest clip-in belts, but Shelby deleted these to add vertical belts that split behind the driver or front passenger's neck and attached at the sides of the seat. This system made rear-seat entry more difficult.

Shelby did add some creature comforts. Dearborn had reported that Mustang customers ordered air-conditioning and automatic transmissions more routinely than not. Fifteen years earlier, Ford management had concluded that shifting gears was something drivers had done before World War II, but Ford's product planners believed buyers

would pay more to let a machine do it. Mustang owners, it appeared, were reaching this same conclusion. Shelby cars used Ford's Deluxe Mustang interior in black or parchment tan (though some cars appeared with white interiors).

When Fred Goodell arrived in September 1966 as Shelby's new chief engineer in charge of assembly, he found mechanics hand-sanding and finishing body panels. Shelby dismissed it, concluding there were "too many racers" on staff still performing the labor-intensive perfection needed to win races. When they dug further, they learned the problem was more serious.

The '67 prototype that Dearborn shipped to Shelby American apparently had suffered some torsional chassis twisting during earlier development work. After carefully

All Shelby road cars were fitted with rear seats in 1967. The parchment interior made its debut in the 1967 model year. C-pillar vents were opened and shut manually from the interior.

drawing fiberglass body pieces according to Ford's plans, McHose, Stacey, and Brock prudently test-fit each prototype piece, frequently revising their plans accordingly before ordering production panels. The result was that many pieces didn't fit the San Jose production bodies, which meant that they required endless hand sanding to fit them to the cars.

Goodell warned Shelby that they needed to set daily production quotas and locate parts that fit properly the first time. Both men felt fiberglass still fit the nature of the car, that the buyers expected it, and that it provided essential economies over stamping 4,000 steel hoods—a relatively small number by Ford's standards. When Goodell went to meet with Shelby's vendors, the fiberglass suppliers in

Southern California surprised him. They could quickly turn out one, two, or three flawless prototypes, but the prospect of manufacturing 4,000 identical pieces in a month caused eyes to glaze over and jaws to go slack. Goodell looked farther and farther from Los Angeles, finally contracting with a company in Canada for the hoods and other fiberglass pieces.

Pete Stacey's center-mounted headlights caused a serious crisis. Goodell learned that no one at Shelby American had cleared this design with California's Department of Motor Vehicles (DMV) or officials from any other state. Properly fitting fiberglass panels presented a bigger problem to solve, and by the time Goodell met with vehicle code compliance people in Sacramento, Shelby

Earlier Shelby road cars used a button on the dash to honk the horn, but by 1967, the steering-wheel hub was handling that duty.

American had already completed close to 200 of the 1967 model cars. Goodell learned that California (and many other states) had strictly prescribed minimum distances that they required between headlights. More seriously, the only vehicles that could operate in any state with red marker lights on their sides were emergency vehicles such as ambulances and fire trucks. They were furious with Shelby and Goodell, accusing them and Ford of "putting stuff out that hasn't been approved by anybody." California's DMV believed that Shelby was "Ford Motor Company in disguise," and not an independent contractor. They ordered the center high beams relocated and the red

lights removed, and if Shelby didn't comply, the DMV promised to "stop [him] from selling cars anywhere."

"Well, I don't have to tell you that we made the necessary changes," Goodell told Dave Friedman. "We changed the grille and moved the headlights." Very few original cars got out of the airport and into local private hands. Goodell made certain that center-headlight cars left California. A good number of those cars still exist. But it's almost impossible to find a car today that still has its high rear marker lights in place.

Shelby American made good on its promise to bring Henry Ford a second victory at Le Mans. The assault team returned to France uniformed in colorful new Mark IV models armed with Shelby's 7-liter engines. Ferrari had kept his endurance team home in Modena in June 1966. He intended this to degrade Ford's victory as less significant since it lacked serious competition. For 1967, Ferrari returned with serious sports-racing 4-liter 330P4 coupes. Two of them snuck in to take second and third behind Shelby's longtime friend Dan Gurney and stock-car-driving champion A. J. Foyt, though the fastest Ferrari was still 53 kilometers (33 miles) back, four laps behind the winner. Shelby's other Ford GT40 Mk IV finished fourth. Ford Division in Dearborn, Ford of France, the Swiss team Scuderia Filipinetti, and John Wyer entered another 10 GTs. In advance of regulations announced for 1968 limiting engine displacement to 5 liters, Wyer campaigned new 5-liter engines in Gulf Oil–sponsored GT40 Mirages, cars based on GT40 Mk Is with narrower and more streamlined cockpits. None of Wyer's cars finished; their unproven engines were not up to the 24-hour challenge.

With Ford's second victory in the history books, Henry Ford II was satisfied and, with millions of dollars

Underneath the twin Holley 659-cubic-feet-per-minute carburetors sat the 428-cubic-inch Police Interceptor engine. An aluminum medium-rise intake manifold helped the big block generate 355 horsepower and a healthy 420 foot-pounds of torque.

invested, he was finished. Ford's own GT program, unwilling to adjust to 5-liter engine restrictions for 1968, ended later that fall and Shelby's programs unwound soon after.

Shelby possessed a second sense about competition priorities with Ford Motor Company. He saw clearly where competitive products fit, and he listened to what kids on the street talked about, lusted after, and saved their money for. That awareness led to yet another rare automobile revered by Shelby enthusiasts.

"I thought I'd seen the ultimate in road car, the Corvette Sting Ray 427," Fred Freel wrote in the August 1967 issue of *Drag Strip* magazine. "Scratch one belief: The new Shelby Snake has it all the way. No reflection on Chevrolet, but this new car . . . could show the Chevy engineers how to go about building a *real* road machine."

Shelby American's Don McCain served as Carroll's West Coast field rep for two years. His primary responsibility was assembling Shelby's Mustang drag cars and assisting customers and racers who bought them. Along with the regular shipments of 428 Interceptor engines that Shelby American received, Carroll occasionally found a 427 Le Mans–configured V-8 on the transporter. He and McCain developed their idea for this car around one of those.

Aggressively tuned 427s produce massive horsepower—more than 600— and comparable torque without much work, but this output renders them nearly unusable on the street. Shelby and McCain chose to start with the endurance-bred 427, select every racing part Ford had available for high-rise manifold versions, and put these in a medium-riser configuration. When they were done, they finished off the engine with an aluminum front engine plate and cylinder heads that lifted 95 pounds off the front end. McCain replaced every part in the engine with pieces

designed for 7,000-rpm performance. When Shelby had used these engines in racing Cobras, he conservatively rated output at 485 brake horsepower. McCain found 360 horsepower at the rear wheels when he put one in a GT500 body on their chassis dynamometer. As writer Fred Freel declared, if you take the Le Mans engine—which is meant for 24-hours of full-throttle acceleration and flat-out running—and you beef up parts from there, "There's no telling how long it will last for street use."

For Shelby, handling was always important. He made small changes for this car. Sitting lighter at the front than the 428-engined GT500, the Super Snake was already more maneuverable. Shelby and McCain added small traction bars to the rear axle to handle what they estimated was an

Left: **Carroll Shelby stretched the nose of the 1967 Shelby road cars by installing a one-piece fiberglass nose that incorporated the grille surround, gravel pan, front-fender extensions, and lower valance. The hood was lengthened to fit as well.** *Right:* **This prototype 1967 GT500 Super Snake used a 427 side-oiler engine to average 142 miles per hour for 500 miles on Goodyear Tire's test track in San Angelo, Texas. At times it reached 170 miles per hour**

extra 160 horsepower on the ground. At Goodyear's Texas high-speed oval, as Freel wrote, "Carroll lapped the track at an easy 150 miles per hour, and when the 427-incher was really turned on, the speedometer tripped the 170 miles per hour mark with ease. . . . At these speeds the engine had to be turning in the neighborhood of 6,000 revs, so the camshaft must be one of those beauties that turns on both at the top end and down where the torque is needed." Long Beach Ford dealer Mel Burns put a $7,500 price tag on it, claiming the cost of the Le Mans 7-liter engine made the car 50 percent more expensive than a 427 Corvette. Apparently it was too pricey. Chevrolet manufactured 20 of its 430-horsepower L-88s in 1967. Shelby produced just one Super Snake.

In early 1965, Don Frey had pulled the European endurance effort from NASCAR specialist Holman Moody and put it in Shelby's hands. It was valuable work for his engineers, mechanics, and racing crews, as well as income for his company. But Shelby understood that Ford moved its racing business around. For 1967, Ford's corporate Trans-Am efforts went with another NASCAR veteran, Bud Moore, who campaigned the new Mercury Cougars in a team effort that Dan Gurney led. Shelby, who was still a racer at heart, couldn't ignore this highly competitive series that he, Jerry Titus, and Ford had won the previous year. He launched his own full-team effort with Titus, Dr. Dick Thompson, and Ronnie Bucknum driving three 1967 notchbacks. Chuck Cantwell remained in place as chief engineer, and Lew Spencer, as team manager, took care of logistics.

Because manufacturers, and not drivers, won the championships, the Trans-Am series had become a key

Above: For the most part, the Super Snake resembled a stock 1967 GT500, but once the accelerator went down, the 427 side-oiler demanded a driver's full attention.

Right: Only one Shelby road car used three Le Mans stripes, the experimental 1967 GT500 Super Snake. Built to evaluate the feasibility of installing the race-bred 427-cubic-inch side-oiler engine, it proved that the famed powerplant would work well in the Shelby.

marketing tool for Chevrolet with its new Camaro, Chrysler with its Plymouth Barracuda and Dodge Dart, AMC with its AMX, and Ford and Mercury with their Mustang and Cougar. Alfa Romeo, BMW, and Porsche fiercely contested the championship in the classes for engines below 2 liters. For the 1967 season, Shelby American assembled 26 Group II Mustangs. It kept four as team cars and sold the others as customer racers. GT350R modifications still kept the cars competitive, and Shelby continued to provide customers with updates and upgrades. Ford Division's involvement with Shelby in the 1967 series was discreet so as not to antagonize Bud Moore with his Mercury contract. Shelby routinely entered his car through Texan David Witts, a friend and lawyer who was his partner in the Terlingua Ranch. The second Shelby car came through Grady Davis, Gulf Oil's racing enthusiast chairman.

A Dodge Dart won the season's first race at Daytona, Jerry Titus in Shelby's Terlingua Racing Team car won the second at Sebring. The third race was the stuff of legends, however. At Green Valley Raceway near Fort Worth, Texas, Titus rolled the car during Friday practice. He crushed the roof, windshield, doors, fenders, and hood. Trans-Am mechanic Bernie Kretschmar recalled the rest of the story for Dave Friedman.

"Jerry came to us with blood running down the side of his face where the windshield had got him, and he said to me and Jerry Schwartz, 'You think you can fix this thing and have it running by tomorrow?' I thought we were done, but we went to town, found the local Ford dealer, and got a brand new Mustang which we immediately stripped of its fenders, hood, and doors. We were up all night straightening the front end."

Kretschmar, Schwartz, and two other mechanics used a hydraulic Porta-Power tool to reshape the roof. They mounted the new fenders, windshield, and doors, and the car made the morning practice. After Titus won the consolation race, Mark Donohue approached Kretschmar and asked him to come to work for Roger Penske, who was running Donohue's Camaros. Kretschmar declined the offer. At the final race of the year, Titus crashed hard again and borrowed John McComb's 1967 car to complete the race weekend and the series. But McComb's engine wasn't up to Titus' pace. Titus failed to even finish, leaving the final victory to teammate Ronnie Bucknum. Between Bucknum, Titus, and Thompson, Shelby's Mustangs had earned points for 15 top-five finishes in the 12 races. Shelby had won again, beating Bud Moore's Mercury Cougar team by two points and Penske's Camaro by seven.

Near the end of 1967 production as Shelby American was gearing up for the 1968 car run, North American Aviation gave Shelby notice on his month-to-month lease of the two large hangars where he ran Shelby American. Because the airport owned the ground beneath the structures, aviation-related businesses held priority and zoning regulations gave that use a higher priority. Shelby had to move. John Kerr and Ray Goodell tried to lease space at Ford's San Jose plant without luck. A contact with Southern Pacific Railroad was willing to build a large structure for them up near San Jose, but the Ford plant manager balked at providing all the cars Shelby American

Left: **Because of the tremendous heat generated by the 427 side-oiler engine, Shelby engineers fitted cooling vents to the fiberglass hood of the Super Snake.**

Above: **After the 1967 GT500 Super Snake had finished its duties at Shelby American, it was put on a lot for sale, priced at $7,500. It sat there for a year before it was purchased.**

After word came down from various states that center-mounted headlights were against regulations, Shelby moved the lamps to the outside of the grille for the rest of the 1967 production run.

would need. He was reluctant to interrupt his tight production schedule as much as Shelby would require.

John Kerr had a friend, George McCellan, working at A. O. Smith in Ionia, Michigan. For a number of years, Smith had assembled Corvettes, but they had just lost that contract. McCellan was very interested, and within months Ford had contracted with A. O. Smith for Shelby Mustang assembly. It proved to be a blessing for Shelby. His production had increased to 3,227 cars for 1967, nearly two-thirds of which were the more luxurious GT500 models. Even with his two huge hangars, he was running out of room. Ford Division saw the situation as an opportunity to bring under tighter control some of the situations that had caused problems with California's DMV (among others). It also knew that it could manufacture Shelby's cars closer to home more efficiently and more profitably with some of the work done as part of its regular assembly-line process. In that way it would save the costs of freight added to each car. With production in nearby Ionia, Ford took quality control supervision in-house.

One other change in Dearborn would develop equal significance, but the cause originated elsewhere. High-performance automobiles had become big business. This trend was initiated by Pontiac Division visionary John DeLorean with the creation of the Tempest GTO in 1963

and was infused and accelerated by Ford's Mustang. The youth market to which it appealed drove many product decisions through the rest of the 1960s. Late in 1967 in downtown Detroit, General Motors' board of directors unwittingly provided fresh ammunition for the performance war when they passed over Semon E. "Bunkie" Knudsen for the position of corporation president.

When Henry Ford II learned that this GM executive might be available, he urged his board to get Knudsen. This required Ford's directors to promote its president, Arjay Miller, to vice chairman to open the post for Knudsen. Bunkie was known throughout the auto industry as an enthusiastic, energetic, product-oriented leader. He had encouraged Chevrolet to develop the newly introduced Camaro and its Trans-Am race-series-inspired Z-28. Lee Iacocca, who had anticipated receiving that job himself because of his success with the Mustang, was surprised and disappointed. But he was also wise enough to know that few things last forever. Knudsen showed up at Ford's world headquarters on February 6, 1968, and promptly set to work. He was intimate with all of GM's plans for future products, and now at Ford, he prepared to unleash a fury of product retribution on his former employer. He didn't mind if he got even with a former competitor at the same time.

"Henry Ford II knew Bunkie's family," Shelby explained. "There were a lot of reasons Henry passed over Iacocca. He resented his publicity consciousness, he didn't think Iacocca was old enough, other things. But Henry would make decisions like that and not even tell his board.

"I knew I was in trouble when I heard Bunkie was coming. Our Cobras and our Mustangs had been beating his Chevrolets and Corvettes for years. Just a week before he got hired, I sent Bunkie a telegram at GM telling him I'd

The 427-cubic-inch side-oiler V-8 fit into the engine compartment of the 1967 GT500 with ease. Its 520 horses weren't handled quite so easily; the rear tires didn't stand a chance.

like to buy one of his automatic transmissions that he had in Jim Hall's Chaparrals.

"He wrote me back, 'Go build your own, you smart son-of-a-bitch.' And then a week later he was the president of the company.

"We weren't making any money with the Mustangs," Shelby continued. "The day Bunkie came in, I told all my guys, 'Shelby is dead with Bunkie Knudsen. Take the Mustangs and do whatever you want with them.'

"And Bunkie decided to put me out of business by building the Bosses."

By the time the year ended, Shelby had manufactured 1,175 GT350 Fastbacks and 2,048 GT500s. In their shops, they had also fabricated a single car as a prototype 1968 GT500 convertible, and one GT500 notchback prototype. This was the car they called Little Red. Its story constitutes yet another Shelby legend.

Carroll came to Fred Goodell one morning, wondering if he could supercharge the 428 Police Interceptor. Goodell was intrigued and found the notchback in the fiberglass shop that mechanics had used earlier in the year to test-fit 1967 body panels. The car was an empty hulk without engine or transmission. With Walter Nelson (Goodell's mechanical chief) in Shelby's experimental garage, they mounted the Paxton on the 428.

They painted it red, gave it a black vinyl roof, and nicknamed it "Little Red." "It was the fastest car that ever ran at Ford's Romeo proving grounds until just recently," Goodell explained to Dave Friedman. "We were pulling 520 brake horsepower and we did 157 miles per hour for 10 miles. That was in 1967." After Little Red had served its purpose, Nelson put the engine on a shelf and Goodell ordered the car cut up and scrapped, one of Ford's prototype rules so no one ever got hurt in a non-production-line automobile.

Projects like Little Red and his Super Snake still excited and inspired Shelby. His season-long campaign in Trans-Am, beating his own bosses and their Cougar team, and winning Le Mans only to be cut loose, were wearing on him. The thrill wasn't gone, but it was looking for a way out.

The interior of the Super Snake was standard GT500. Stock Mustang seats didn't offer much in the way of lateral support, but few sporty automobiles did.

CHAPTER FIVE

KR STANDS FOR "KING OF THE ROAD": 1968

Above: The standard 15-inch wheel covers on the 1968 GT350 replicated the look of a five-spoke alloy wheel.

Right: For 1968, Shelby used a fiberglass panel, painted argent, to surround the 1965 Thunderbird-derived taillights. These were sequential except in the state of California. The Cobra Jet pop-open gas cap was standard.

FOR 1968, SHELBY'S MUSTANGS CHANGED IN SEV-
ERAL WAYS. As Carroll began to extricate himself from
Mustang operations, he sold the "Cobra" name to Ford for
one dollar, while retaining his own unlimited rights to use
it in the future. Because Ford now had access to the name
"Cobra," all Shelby Mustang promotion referred to the cars
as the Cobra GT350 and Cobra GT500. Shelby's name
disappeared from much of the release information that
emerged from Ford that year.

The shift to Michigan assembly furthered the identity
evolution that Shelby had advanced with the 1967
California cars. His first pony cars had been aptly named as
Mustangs. The 1965 cars struck buyers as skittish, untamed
animals that could be saddle-broken but might not like it.
By 1968, the breed hadn't exactly become Kentucky

Walkers, and though they'd gained
weight and added big torquey engines,
they certainly weren't Clydesdales;
these cars were more akin to American
Quarter Horses, reliable, comfortable
long-distance rides with enough agility
to still provide excitement.

The principal cause for this
change lay with new steel hoods. A. O.
Smith had discovered that it cost barely 20 percent more to
use matched-metal dies to stamp hoods (that needed no
hand reworking) than Shelby had spent on fiberglass hoods
imported from Canada and individually fit to each car. The
hoods also sported new horizontal-slit hood scoops near
the nose of the car that were the most efficient yet. Airflow

Above: **One of Carroll Shelby's personal cars waits in the desert for a chance to chase the wind. As good as the styling on the '68 Mustang was, the Shelby version pushed the envelope.**

Opposite page: **Rectangular Marchall 656/322 driving lights were installed in the grille to visually balance the front-end treatment, as well as provide 45,000-candlepower illumination.**

With production shifted to Michigan, Ford found a Canadian source for the fiberglass hood. Functional scoops on the leading edge of the hood take advantage of the ram effect at speed to force ambient air into the engine compartment.

over and through a car body did not always respond the way human intuition predicted. Aerodynamic engineers had learned how to turn the beautiful prototype GT40s into stable, ultra-high-speed racers. Ford's wind-tunnel engineers had learned that air striking the front of the car rose abruptly. It passed over center hood scoops, and while intakes at the base of the windshield benefited from a low-pressure area there, the other location for forced air induction was right up front.

Ford stylists redesigned Shelby's hood-pin-and-clip closure system into flat, finger-operated Dzus fittings, another engineering carry-over from the GT40 racers. This change eliminated the projecting pins and the clips that, to avoid losing them, Shelby wire-strung to the grille. In one of the first evidences of cross-pollination between Shelby and mainstream production models, the same hood closures appeared on Mach I Mustangs as well.

Ford stylists slightly opened the grille and, after fitting

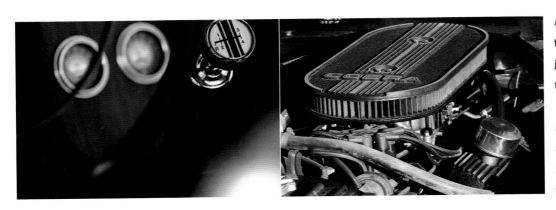

Left: Attention to detail can set a car apart from the rest of the pack, and Shelby never missed an opportunity to do just that. The shift knob on the 1968 GT350 shows Shelby's famed Le Mans stripes, recalling past racing success.

Right: For 1968, the small block in the GT350 grew to a 302-cubic-inch displacement, while horsepower came in at 250. Emissions regulations started to rein in the power in the pursuit of cleaner air.

single headlights near the fender edges to accomplish both high- and low-beam functions, the larger grille looked empty. Chastened by the scolding it received from state governments, Ford confirmed legality before installing rectangular fog lamps from French manufacturer S. E. V. Marchall. U.S. vehicle codes, which had allowed cars of the late 1960s to reach top speeds well above 100 miles per hour, still restricted automakers to a 1939 standard of 35,000 candlepower of front illumination. Shelby knew his Cobra Coupes and GT40s ran with more than 150,000 candlepower at Le Mans and some rally cars used six or eight lights that put out 250,000 candlepower. Patiently working through channels, Shelby, Ford, and Smith got a pair of 35,000-candlepower fog lights legally installed,

effectively doubling his cars' illumination. By mid-year however, Marchal lights were failing. Shelby and Ford switched to English Lucas lamps and replaced a number of failed units under warranty.

Under the hood, the blurring of product lines was more profound. Dictated in part by new U.S.-government emission standards, Ford discontinued the 4.7-liter 289 engine series. Another motivation for the change was the ongoing gentrification of the Shelby Mustangs in which the amount of valvetrain noise from the engine's solid lifters was no longer acceptable. The new 5-liter 302-cubic-inch V-8, with its rectangular valve ports, or "tunnel ports," used hydraulic valve lifters that not only were quieter but also needed less attention and adjustment. Hydraulic-lifter

Side and C-pillar scoops on the 1968 GT350 and GT500 were carried over unchanged from 1967. Suspension modifications from standard Mustangs included high-rate front coil springs, heavy-duty four-leaf rear springs, and high-capacity shock absorbers.

Side-marker lights came on the automotive scene in 1968, as seen on this GT500. Under the long hood lurked a 428-cubic-inch engine, rated at 335 horsepower.

The hood-extractor vents originally seen on the 1967 Super Snake were put into production on the 1968 GT350 and 500. The famed Cobra snake was affixed to the front fender in an attempt to capitalize on the Cobra name.

engines, however, cannot tolerate engine speeds nearly as high as the solid-lifter versions, and, according to Wallace Wyss in *Shelby's Wildlife*, where Shelby had rated the 289 at 306 horsepower at 6,000 rpm, the new engine first appeared rated at 235 horsepower at 4,800 rpm. But Ford quickly revised the number up to 250 horsepower. Initial torque readings were 318 foot-pounds at 3,200 rpm, re-rated down to 310 at 2,800 rpm. This engine, more docile and much quieter, was 56 horsepower and 19 foot-pounds of torque down on performance from the tried-and-true 289. Changing from the Holley 715-cubic-feet-per-minute

four-barrel carburetor to a smaller 600-cubic-feet-per-minute Holley contributed to this milder performance. But to Ford's product planners, the GT350 packages had almost become an afterthought. With the more powerful, more luxurious GT500 model selling nearly twice as many models, planners looked at the lower-output model as the entry-level Shelby, while repeat customers or those they pulled from Corvettes wanted to step up to the greater comfort at the top.

Another way to regain horsepower returned to option books. Shelby offered Paxton's superchargers either

Handsome lines and promises of high performance helped Shelby sell more than 4,400 GT350s and GT500s in 1968. Legend has it that Shelby used the number 500 for the big-block model because it was larger than anyone else's.

installed or available over-the-counter. If Shelby's assemblers in Michigan did the job, they deleted air conditioning because the superchargers were mounted where the air-conditioner compressor would have been located. Those who lived in climates that permitted it and who opted for the supercharger got their performance back. Shelby rated the Supercharged 302 at 335 brake horsepower at 5,200 rpm and torque at 325 foot-pounds at 3,200 rpm.

There was another climate-control option for 1968. In both GT350 and GT500 models, Shelby now offered a convertible. Ford engineers barely had to revise the stock convertible top and Shelby's integral roll bar so the soft top fit over the bar. In a masterpiece of styling and engineering, the Shelby convertibles looked as handsome with the top up as they did with it down. Introducing the convertible proved to be a wise marketing decision, because at the end of 1968, 1,124 buyers had gone for the open cars, and 3,323 buyers opted for coupes.

Ford began the model year continuing the 428 Police Interceptor engine, rated at 360 horsepower at 5,400 rpm and 420 foot-pounds of torque at 3,200 rpm, fitted with the Holley 715-cubic-foot-per-minute four-barrel. At some point

Blurred surroundings came standard with the 1968 Shelby GT500. The Shelby-installed roll bar is visible, as is the folding rear seat that came on the Mustang.

Drama on wheels. Shelby used fiberglass pieces to make up the effective rear spoiler, as well as the taillight surround panel.

in assembly, a shortage of these engines forced A. O. Smith to substitute Ford's 390. According to the *Shelby American World Registry*, it was a well-kept secret. Apparently only a few cars were affected, dealers weren't informed, and the only way to determine today whether a 390 or 428 is in a car is by tearing the engine down to visually inspect part numbers.

For those for whom even 360 horsepower was inadequate, Shelby still got a few of the 427 engines. Dealers tried to discourage buyers from ordering it, but Smith assembled somewhere around 50 of these cars.

Wallace Wyss wrote that, "The 427 had been tamed somewhat as well with hydraulic lifters. . . ." however "tamed" is relative. Ford still rated the engine conservatively at 400 horsepower at 5,600 rpm with 460 foot-pounds of torque at 3,200 rpm. Using a new "cathedral-float" 600-cubic-feet-per-minute four-barrel Holley carburetor, the engine retained sufficient power to shred its standard Goodyear Speedway 130 E70-15 tires on an enthusiastic Saturday night.

Ford/A. O. Smith/Shelby offered automatic and top-loader four-speed transmissions for each engine in both body styles. Ford delivered the four-speed GT350 with a

3.89:1 final drive. The big engines, whether equipped with the three-speed C4 automatic or the manual four speed, came first with 3.25:1 and subsequently with 3.50:1 final drives. Buyers could order performance axles ranging from 4.11:1 or 4.25:1 for no extra cost, or a 4.56:1 for an additional charge beyond frequent refueling expenses. Ford carried over its optional No-Spin that Shelby had introduced in 1966 to replace the standard-equipment (and much noisier) Detroit Locker.

Midway through the 1968 model year, Shelby introduced its GT500KR. The "KR" suffix stood for King of the Road, an appropriate if cocky title for the Mustang fitted with Ford's 428 Cobra-Jet V-8. The mid-year introduction resulted from a trio of considerations. A. O. Smith encountered delays in establishing Shelby assembly in its Ionia facility; Ford endured early model-year production strikes at the Metuchen, New Jersey, plant where Ionia's cars originated; and Ford experienced delays in federalizing the new engine. This probably permanently derailed plans to offer a supercharged version of the KR. The name, however, may also represent a big dose of Shelby skullduggery. According to Wallace Wyss, "Shelby spies discovered that GM was planning to use the same name for their new 396-cubic-inch Camaro, and since Shelby's flexibility of response was quicker, he decided to tweak the tiger's tail by bringing out

a model with the same name before GM could get their project together."

The Cobra Jet was a tiger in its own right. Essentially, it was the existing 428 block but with many important improvements. New cylinder heads came with rectangular exhaust and intake ports, larger than Ford's engineers had used on the 427 Le Mans and factory drag-race engines. Ford's foundry cast the block using higher-grade nodular iron, similar to what it used for the racing 427s. Pistons were alloy, connecting rods were high-strength steel, and two different cams were available, one for normal street

For 1968, both low- and high-beam duties were handled by a single outboard headlight. By the time the GT500KR debuted, the troublesome Marchall fog lights had been replaced with more reliable Lucas units.

The Klik pin hood-restraint system was replaced in 1968 with quick-twist Dzus fasteners. Experience with these in the GT40 program led Shelby to adopt them for his road cars.

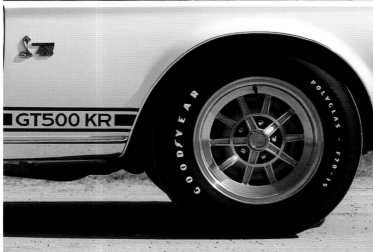

Above: In the latter half of 1968, Shelby introduced the GT500KR, short for King of the Road. All were fitted with FE-based 428 Cobra Jet engines. The late introduction kept production of the convertible to only 318 units.

Left: Space was at a premium in the engine compartment of the 1968 GT500. Displacing 428 cubic inches, the power plant breathed through a single Holley carburetor and was rated at 355 horsepower.

Red and aggressive. The Cobra Jet engine in the 1968 GT500KR was woefully underrated at 335 horsepower; the games with manufacturers and insurance companies had already started.

For fair-weather cruising, it doesn't get much better than a 1968 GT500KR. A roll bar supplied safety as well as stiffened the chassis.

use and the other for drag racing.

Car Life magazine was one of the first to get a KR fastback to test. Ford had to delay writer Allan Girdler's test a few days, however, because thieves stole the test car from the Ford public relations department's parking lot. That prompted the review story headline, "Shelby's Cobra GT500KR—Was it Worth Stealing?"

"The KR's invincibility doesn't matter," Girdler wrote. "The car is so impressive, so intimidating to challengers, that there are no challengers. The KR breeds confidence bordering on arrogance. The KR driver coasts along, mighty

engine rumbling, and looks with a condescending smile on the driver of a lesser car who creeps away from the lights, knuckles white on the steering wheel.

"Carroll Shelby might not be a prisoner in the Ford works, but every year the Shelby Mustang is a little less Shelby, and a little more Mustang," Girdler continued. "The Shelby is thoroughbred Mustang. We might wish for more: a new suspension, maybe; and rear bucket seats meant to be sat in, not climbed out of; and an adjustable steering column instead of that tilt-away thing that goes *whang* at the driver's chin when the door is opened. But the King of

the Road will wow the neighbors, cover ground, and make drivers of ordinary Mustangs eat their hearts out. Well worth stealing."

Hot Rod magazine's Steve Kelly got both a KR fastback and KR convertible to test. His story appeared in November 1968, and his comments pointed out how an automaker would eliminate one customer's complaints only to earn another's dissatisfaction.

"Had it not been for Carroll Shelby's 1965–66 series GT350, with its worthwhile features as a sports and performance machine, Ford probably wouldn't be marketing the current breed of GT350s and GT500s. Nor is it likely that any such car would've developed. Who knows, FoMoCo may not even *like* perpetuating the brand, but they are, and with greater success than when control was in Shelby's hands." While Kelly recognized its origin and appreciated the evolution, he came away confused by the new model's purpose and disappointed with its performance, especially as he compared it to a Corvette comparably equipped and priced.

"There are some who'd say the Shelby car makes more sense [than the Corvette] 'cause it'll hold four people. Well, okay. But for how long and how far? Try running between Los Angeles and San Francisco with two good friends in the back of that fastback Mustang. That'll decide true friendship.

"The KR series Shelby Mustangs are built to attract a wide variety of tastes and interests, which accounts for their stable sales picture. Some sports car customers don't care to sit an inch off the ground, and that is why they don't buy the 'Vette. . . . The Shelby GT500KR may be a better sports vehicle than the production Mustang, but this Ford appears to fall short of the 'Vette. We're bound to get a stack of mail on this one. Better warn the mail room what to expect." Kelly accurately portrayed the evolution occurring in the minds of buyers and product planners as to just what an American sports car was--or could be.

121

When the GT500KR hit the streets, Shelby made sure that drivers in its wake knew that the boisterous vehicle was packing a Cobra Jet engine. The flip-cap was functional.

Car Life got its KR fastback from 0–60 miles per hour in 6.9 seconds and through the standing-start quarter mile in 14.57 seconds at 99.55 miles per hour. *Hot Rod*, by removing accessory belts and the air filter, shortened their quarter-mile times to 14.04 at 102.73 miles per hour. Each magazine's test coupe carried a list price of $4,857, while *Car Life*'s convertible went for $5,350.

Few magazines examined Shelby's 1968 models. With its minimal exterior changes, most GT350s and GT500s got shuffled off the pages by redesigned Corvettes, Dodge's new Charger and Coronet Super-Bee, American Motors Corporation's (AMC) Javelin and AMX, new bodies on Oldsmobile mid-size Cutlasses, four engines for Plymouth's Barracuda, and Pontiac's restyled GTO. Only *Road & Track* magazine tested Shelby's GT350, in its June 1968 issue, just pages in front of its Camaro Z-28 review.

"In 1968, the cycle is almost complete," an unidentified author wrote. "The GT350 now weights over 3,300 lbs., requires power steering for parking and, in basic form, should be considered a Mustang with a racy-looking trim package." The magazine, a longtime admirer of things Shelby, was disillusioned, concluding, "Perhaps the fairest summary of these cars would be to say IF they're the sort of car to which you are attracted, they do the job well enough."

This was sharp judgment from America's automotive magazine of record. Its track tests produced surprising results, albeit accomplished with a 4.11:1 rear axle: 0–60 miles per hour took 6.3 seconds, and its standing-start quarter-mile came in 14.9 at 94 miles per hour. *Road & Track*'s test car had a base price of $4,287 but with enough options that, at $5,368, it cost $18 more than *Hot Rod*'s GT500KR convertible!

While magazine reviews such as these disappointed Shelby and Ford's public-relations staffs, product planners and others higher up the management chain paid much more attention to the dealers. It was they who constituted the company's most vocal critics and who had Dearborn's closest ear.

When the KR appeared, Ford rated it, like the Police Interceptor before it, at 335 horsepower at 5,200 rpm and 440 foot-pounds of torque at 3,400 rpm. Magazine

Automobile headlights of the 1960s were limited to a 1939 standard output of 35,000 candlepower. It didn't take a very heavy foot to outdrive them in a GT500KR.

A large-displacement engine requires large volumes of air, and the functional hood scoop on the 1968 GT500KR worked like a charm. With the introduction of emissions controls, engine compartments would start to resemble bowls of spaghetti.

reviewers and customers quickly questioned what rating scale Ford had been using when tire-spinning starts were harder to avoid than accomplish. Insurance companies were becoming increasingly effective in their own forms of automobile product planning. For clients with bad driving records, underwriters raised rates so drastically that some customers spent as much or more for coverage than they spent to buy the automobile. Ford dealers already had cancelled orders from Shelby customers when they couldn't get insurance for their new cars. Under-rating engine output might throw off insurance companies, but drag-racing sanctioning bodies knew better and simply re-rated the engine closer to where they knew it ran: Between 410 and 425 horsepower.

At the end of 1967, seven months before *Road & Track* ran its review, Carroll Shelby stopped in at the magazine's offices to bring them up to date on the business

and new developments. Moving production from Los Angeles to Michigan led to a restructuring of Shelby's operations. Shelby American became Shelby Automotive, with its main office at A. O. Smith's facility in Ionia. Shelby Racing moved from its former hangars at 6501 West Imperial Highway to an 84,000-square-foot building a few miles farther south of the airport on 190th Street in Torrance, California. Shelby's other business, Shelby Parts, started life in the Torrance facility, handling all aftermarket parts and accessories for Mustangs. By mid-year Shelby Parts moved to Ionia, Michigan, becoming Shelby Autosports. Carroll had purchased a four-story office building in Playa del Rey, a short walk from his old hangars. He had ended all U.S. production of the Ford-engined A.C.-bodied Cobras, due, he explained, to U.S. safety regulations. "Meeting them requires too much engineering time."

Le Mans stripes tucked underneath the front valance of the GT500KR. With 445 foot-pounds of torque, getting the rear tires to hook up was a driver's biggest problem.

Letting a GT500KR loose on the drag strip resulted in good numbers, especially for a vehicle that tipped the scale at close to 2 tons. The beefy Shelby ran the quarter-mile in 14.57 seconds at 99.56 miles per hour. It recorded a 0–60 mile-per-hour time of 6.9 seconds.

He already had a new prototype in development at Torrance, his Cobra replacement called the Lone Star. This was a curvaceous, mid-engined coupe with a removable Targa-type roof on a 92.8-inch wheelbase, measuring 161 inches long overall and 40 inches high, and weighing just 2,040 pounds with the 289. Shelby made it clear to *Road & Track* editors that the car would not accommodate the 427. While its racing roots and its potential were apparent, the prototype also had electric side windows and a full interior. The editors asked if he planned to produce it.

"Only if the government decides to exempt small car makers. . . ." Carroll told them. "If not, I'll quit. But I'm not crying. Production was taking too much of my time anyway." That much was true. Shelby was far from bored and inactive. He had begun preparing three Toyota 2000 GTs for SCCA C-production, he was working on a Can-Am effort with Len Terry in England, and he had won back Ford's full backing as its factory Trans-Am team for 1968. That project, however, would bring enough disappointments to alter Shelby's outlook for years.

Douglas Waschenko, writing in the *Shelby American World Registry,* pointed out that the SCCA Trans-Am series

"had struck a nerve with motorsports fans across the United States. . . . The SCCA was wise enough to realize that if they allowed competitors to modify their cars to the point where they were no longer recognizable, fans would lose interest in the series in direct proportion." The popularity of Trans-Am and NASCAR was based on enthusiasts rooting for "cars just like they drove."

The Trans-Am series, for many automobile enthusiasts, also changed their definition of sports car. Before Trans-Am, sports cars were typically open two-seated cars. Most came from Europe, with the exception of Chevrolet's

Corvettes and a few other limited-production American species such as Cunninghams and Kaiser-Darrins. Shelby's GT350, as Waschenko said, "stretched the definition of sports car," and the SCCA gave it their blessing. A year later, the same organization broadened the definition with a Trans-Am series that required four seats. Now the car on the track was much more like the car the enthusiasts drove to work.

Shelby Racing produced five new 1968 cars for the season and updated the strongest two 1967 cars to 1968 SCCA specs. These regulations allowed engines to be bored to the full 5-liter 305-cubic-inch displacement, with 8-inch wheel widths inside flared and widened fenders, creating a minimum weight for Shelby's class of 2,800 pounds. These were easy conversions, and Shelby chose not to assemble a new series of customer cars but simply to prepare and enter two of his cars in each event.

The 24-hour opener at Daytona went according to Shelby's plan. Jerry Titus and Ronnie Bucknum won the Trans-Am class following three prototype Porsche 907 long-tail pure race cars across the finish line. At that point, Ford Division took over managing the effort. Ford insisted on using the 440-horsepower engines that Shelby's personnel could only install but not modify. The remainder of the 13-race series embarrassed Shelby and Ford's engine department. The new tunnel-port race-tuned engines had a narrow power band from 7,000 to 8,000 rpm. Oil failed to reach the right places at those speeds. Worse still, engine assembly problems were appalling, which rumors of soured labor relations at the plants may explain. Shelby crew members reported uncrating new engines, and under the scrutiny of watchful Ford engineers, removing valve covers to discover engines missing pushrods or valve rocker arms. Team manager Lew Spencer came to define race weekends as four-engine or six-engine races, referring to the number that would fail on Friday, Saturday, and Sunday. By mid-season, Shelby's crew members had started a pool betting on which race lap an engine would let go.

Rules specifically prohibited modification from original specifications, and Ford adamantly denied Shelby's requests to build his own engines, so Phil Remington devised a way to hide a dry-sump oil pan *inside* the deeper wet sump. Engines began to last through shorter races and Titus won the 2 1/2-hour event at Watkins Glen. Still, in 12 of the 13 events, at least one of the 302-powered Mustangs did not finish the race. Horst Kwech had replaced Bucknum beginning with the fifth race and he and Titus labored through the remainder of the season. Titus was so frustrated that he left Shelby before the final race and put together a team of Pontiac Firebirds for 1969. Roger Penske, driver Mark Donohue, and Chevrolet's Camaro Z-28 won the championship. AMC's Javelin had made an aggressive show, and if anyone needed further evidence of the promotional value manufacturers placed on Trans-Am victory, rumors circulated that American Motors had offered Penske $2 million to run their program.

Few of Titus' teammates could blame him for leaving, and some wondered if Shelby had entertained similar thoughts about his relationship with Ford. Cobra GT production for 1968 set a new record out of the Ionia facility. Ford manufactured 4,450 Cobra GT350s, GT500s, and GT500KRs. It was nearly a 35-percent increase over 1967. Fastbacks outnumbered convertibles nearly three to one, 3,326 to 1,124, and big-blocks outsold the 302s by nearly two to one, 2,793 to 1,657.

(For those keeping track, while Ford had officially withdrawn from the GT40 program and racing at Le Mans,

Far left: **Conelec fuel injection systems provided an experimental system that proved temperamental. Eventually, a conventional induction system was installed.**

Left: **Since the Mustang's earliest days, independent rear suspension was considered. Shelby installed a system underneath the EXP 500 within the existing space. Beefy tubular arms ensured durability.**

Above: Shelby built a 1968 coupe into an experimental test-bed for two engineering exercises. Nicknamed the "Green Hornet" due to its color and the comic-strip character of the same name, it was scheduled to be crushed, but it was able to evade that fate.

Right: Polyglas tires and a 429 Cobra Jet engine—it wasn't much of a contest. When experiments with Conelec fuel injection were concluded, a 428CJ engine was slipped in.

Reflecting its special status, the EXP 500's rocker stripes were two-tone. No Shelby coupe road cars were ever built with intent for public sale.

Inset: The rubber skirt on top of the 1968 428CJ's air-cleaner housing fit against the bottom of the hood, allowing air from the hood scoop to be fed directly into the induction system.

Factory air conditioning was one of the many creature comforts fitted to the 1968 EXP 500 Green Hornet engineering study. Vehicles used for evaluation purposes were usually crushed to avoid any legal entanglements later if the automobile were to get into the hands of the public.

The 1968 EXP 500 was the only Shelby built with a vinyl roof. Intended as a high-performance Grand Touring vehicle, it was equipped with a full slate of options.

Shelby's longtime friends John Wyer from his Aston Martin days and Grady Davis, a steady racing sponsor as Gulf Oil's chairman, took over the effort. The French autoclub ran Le Mans in September that year due to student protests in May that led to a national strike of virtually all industry in June. Wyer's Gulf GT40 Mk II led two new prototype Porsches across the line. The nearest Ferrari finished seventh.)

For Carroll Shelby, 1969 would be another year of ups and downs. Ford had promised new 302 engines for racing, and the company renewed his contract for the 1969 Trans-Am season. The company's new president, Bunkie Knudsen, arrived February 6 and was quickly shaking things up. Ford had new sheet metal for the Mustang. Knudsen had brought with him stylist Larry

Shinoda. While they each had arrived too late to influence this year greatly, they assured Shelby his car would look most distinctive for 1969. Even as Knudsen's Bosses competed with Shelby's GT350 and GT500 models, Ford marketing recognized the Shelby name value and returned it to the GTs.

But Ford Division also hedged its bets. It engaged Bud Moore, who had run Cougars in 1967, to manage a second official Ford Division Trans-Am team in 1969. And from its own product planners, Ford advanced a lineup of Mustangs that competed with what Shelby's cars had become. The words from magazine car reviewers and motorsports journalists the year before had stung, but they mattered little. Shelby paid more attention to the words of his boss, Henry Ford II.

CHAPTER SIX

POWERED BY FORD, BUILT BY FORD: 1969

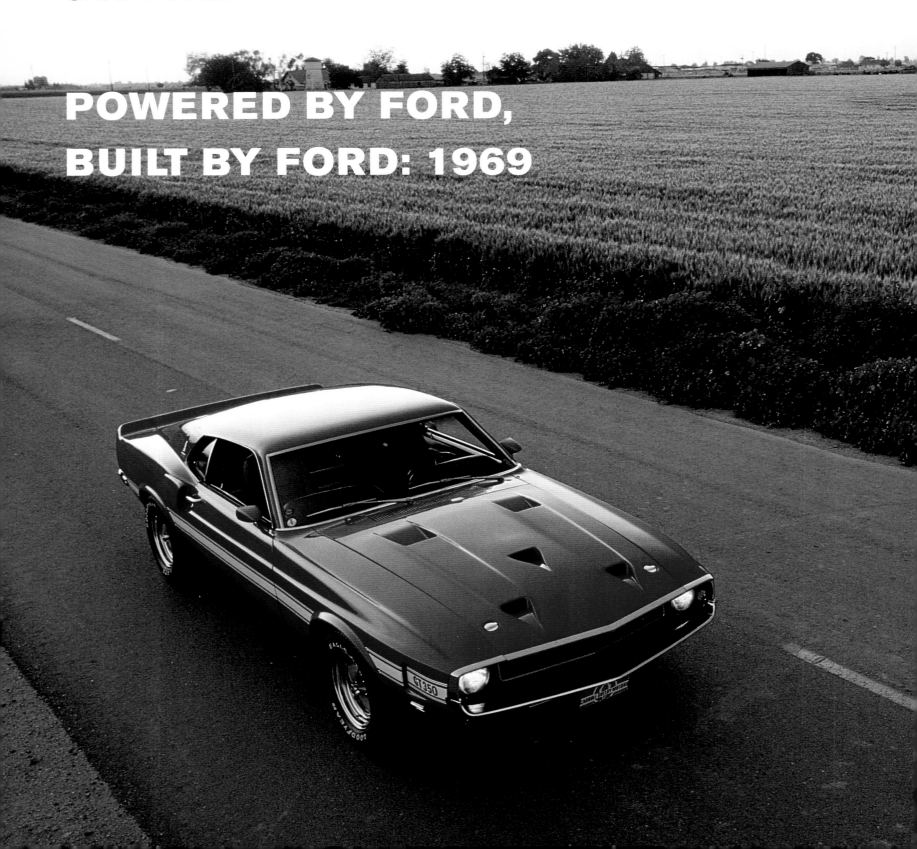

Left: **No longer built for competing on tight racetracks, the 1969 Shelbys were more at home on the open road—the straighter the better.**

Below: **Production Mustang Mach 1s used faux scoops behind the doors, but being a Shelby, they were functional, directing air to the rear drum brakes. A bolt-in roll bar was part of the Shelby package.**

IT TOOK 21 SEPARATE PIECES OF PLASTIC AND FIBERGLASS TO REMODEL AND RESHAPE THE BODY OF THE GT350 AND GT500 FOR 1969. Bunkie Knudsen and Larry Shinoda had been true to their words. Shelby's Mustangs were more distinctive for the new model year. The fiberglass panels came from Owens-Corning, a company familiar to Knudsen and competent in fiberglass manufacture after years of working with Chevrolet on the Corvettes. One look at the cars made it clear that Ford Division's emphasis now was on appearance. All that remained of regular-production Mustangs were the roof and the two doors. Everything else was freshly created by Shelby's stylists on loan from Ford Design.

What had been subtle in the past became almost flamboyant. Designers sliced five National Advisory Committee on Aeronautics (NACA) ducts into the hood, three to maneuver air into the air cleaner and two to evacuate heat from the engine compartment. Ford's designers had used some of their first ones on Ford's GT-40 FIA Appendix J-prototype, the legendary J-car, adopting them from jet aircraft technology. Since the late 1930s, General Motors had introduced design and engineering features in the highest divisions—the most elite and exclusive product lines—that led the way in following years for lesser models to follow. Bordinat and his staff sensed from Knudsen's style and Shinoda's work that the GT350/GT500 design would influence the next generation

Above: The 1969 Shelby road cars' lineage was evident in a profile. Ford's Mustang now had a SportsRoof model rather than a fastback, so Shelby worked the design to be even more flamboyant than the Mach 1. *Inset:* Center-mounted exhaust tips were made of aluminum and tended to quickly become covered with soot. Shelby continued using 1965 Thunderbird taillights.

Opposite page: The full-width grille housed a pair of headlights and the requisite Shelby logo. Lucas driving lamps underneath the Shelby-exclusive bumper kicked out 70,000 candlepower.

Luxury touches abounded in the 1969 GT350, as befits a Grand Touring vehicle. Genuine simulated teakwood appliqués warmed up the interior.

For 1969, the grille-mounted Shelby logo returned to the driver's side. Due to the 4-inch lengthening of the fiberglass hood, the fiberglass front fenders were stretched as well.

Over time, the hood springs tended to bow the fiberglass hood, creating a gap with the fenders. Shelby took a page from the GT40 program that used NACA ducts for airflow management.

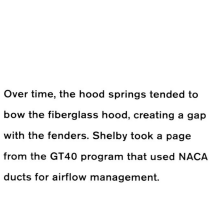

Above: Never designed to blend in with the crowd, the 1969 GT350 stood out in an era of stand-out musclecars. Ford stylists worked with the Shelby staff to create a vehicle significantly different from its Mustang cousin.

Left: Front fender scoops were intended to feed cooling air to the front disc brakes. How effective they were is a matter of conjecture. The impact-susceptible nose required a deft touch to parallel park.

Above: Looking like it's accelerating while standing still, the 1969 GT500's slight nose-up attitude exuded a purposeful air. Huge C-pillars compromised rearward visibility.

Opposite page: One of Carroll Shelby's personal cars basks in the sun, roll-bar-mounted inertia-reel shoulder harnesses visible hanging down. The width of the grille emphasized the aggressive stance.

of Mustangs. They changed nomenclature. Ford now called its fastback roof the SportsRoof. Staff designers tested other Shelby appearance cues on auto-show crowds through Ford dream cars. The 1970 Mustang Milano bore several elements adopted from Shelby's cars. These cues would strongly influence the final look of the 1971 production Mustang. This included not only the ducts but also the wide, flat, rectangular grille opening.

Ford set aside the 302 with its 220 brake horsepower and installed the 290-horsepower 351-cubic-inch V-8 that the division assembled at its Windsor, Ontario, engine-assembly plant. The 351 was a next-step development of the 289 and many performance parts were available.

Horsepower peak arrived at 4,800 rpm while its hefty 385 foot-pounds of torque peaked at 3,400 rpm. Ford mounted an Autolite 550-cubic-feet-per-minute four-barrel on an aluminum high-rise manifold.

The GT500 carried over the 428 Cobra Jet (CJ), still rated at 335 horsepower with Holley four-barrels on its medium-rise intake manifolds. Product planners went through several discussions about whether to continue calling the CJ-models King of the Road. Shortly before production started, the KR designation slipped off the car and sank from sight. Suspension for the cars carried over the Mustang Mach I configuration, using Gabriel Adjust-O-Matic shock absorbers and Goodyear F60-15 Polyglas bias-belted tires. But prices had to come up, adjusted by marketing's decisions to make more options mandatory in order to configure the car as a Shelby—the way Ford wanted to sell it. The GT350 SportsRoof started at $4,434, with a similarly adorned GT500 going for $4,700. Of course, dealers who would receive only a single model of each Shelby per year loaded up their versions with options. While it increased everyone's profits, dealers found buyers ready to have every creature comfort and willing to pay for it. Fully equipped GT500 convertibles wore a sticker price in excess of $6,300. Few of these customers were baby-boomers but many were their parents. With children finishing college, they were able for the first time to enjoy the rewards of their hard work and the abundance of a healthy economy.

An interesting image evolution had taken place as well. Ford's official photos of the Cobra GT350 and GT500 models for 1968 showed women in evening formal attire. It was clear to anyone who saw these beautifully lit black-and-white studio photos that this Mustang was no longer the bruiser GT350 of 1965. It was a stylishly developed Grand Tourer as capable of driving through Detroit's suburban Grosse Pointe Woods, Chicago's North Shore, or California's Beverly Hills on the way to any black-tie soiree. For 1969, the models, still women, wore pantsuits or miniskirts. Sport and Shelby were back together.

Convertibles and SportsRoof models retained their integral padded roll bars, and the enclosed cars kept the two-piece shoulder harnesses introduced with the 1967 and '68 models. By 1969, the nature of the Shelby Mustang had changed drastically. It had been Shelby's 1965 and '66 racing homologation specials that *Car and Driver* writer Steve Smith had characterized as "a brand-new, clapped-out race car." For 1967 and '68, Shelby and Ford offered the cars in a broad range of exterior colors, and by 1969 and '70, product planners and marketing experts made sure

With this alphanumeric designation on the front fender, the engine compartment was filled with a 428 Cobra Jet engine. This potent powerplant delivered 335 horsepower, at least on paper.

The snake motif would survive on the sides of high-performance Mustangs long after the cessation of production of Shelby road cars. Ford owned the logo, and they would get mileage from it for many years.

It's doubtful we'll see engine displacements this large again, as electronics now coax similar amounts of power from far smaller engines. One advantage of cubic inches is prodigious torque, in this case 440 foot-pounds of twist.

Above: **The full-length tape stripe down the flanks of the GT500 was made of a material that would reflect light in the dark.**

Right: **Three of the five NACA ducts on the hood of the 1969 GT500 ingested air, while the aft pair drew out hot air.**

there were abundant choices for interior options as well. The cars came completely carpeted and trimmed with chrome. Ford's interior designers applied imitation teak wood to the center console, door panels, and dash. The power-roof convertible dropped effortlessly into a cavity where a vinyl boot covered it with little effort. As Wallace Wyss pointed out, Cadillac's Eldorado had used the same system for several years: Here was another instance where Knudsen introduced something from the highest division and its most exclusive models to begin its trickle-down influence.

Shelby's Mustangs now wore the full array of regular production Ford Mustang colors. While interiors and tops only came in black or white, exterior colors came in Gulfstream Aqua, Acapulco Blue, Grabber Blue, Grabber Red, Candy Apple Red, Silver Jade, Pastel Gray, Black, Black Jade, Royal Maroon, Wimbledon White, and Pink. Appropriately, Connie Kreski, *Playboy* magazine's

With the increased emphasis on comfort, even in sports cars, it was inevitable that Shelby road cars would ladle on the options, creating a comfortable long-haul cruiser.

Not an environment that was conducive to long travel, the fold-down rear seats fulfilled the requirement of the vehicle being a four-seater in spirit, if not in fact. The steeply raked backlight limited headroom.

23-year-old Playmate of the Year for 1969, received a pink Shelby GT500 SportsRoof as part of her prize package.

The interior had grown more Grand Turismo in appearance and comforts. Large instruments faced the driver (and canted toward him or her) and included an integrated 140-mile-per-hour speedometer, an 8,000-rpm tachometer, a water-temperature gauge, an oil-pressure gauge, and an ammeter. Toggle switches below the instruments operated the Lucas quartz-iodide 70,000 candlepower driving lights mounted below the grille at the front of the car.

For 1969, the GT350 sold for $4,434, about $100 below the spartan 1965 model. Ford published a $4,700 base price for the GT500. In truth, few if any cars left dealer lots in base configuration. As the Ford family grew, some dealers had trouble getting even a single Shelby to

sell, so if they did, they plumped it with options. It was possible to see a window sticker at $5,500 for a GT350 and as much as $6,300 for a GT500 convertible.

Not only had prices and overall dimensions increased over the years but, against all of Shelby's inclinations, so had weight. Between air conditioners and power-roof mechanisms, air pumps and heavy-duty batteries, a GT350 now weighed 3,689 pounds.

A study of production numbers for 1969 Shelby Mustangs revealed a few interesting variations. According to Vincent Liska in the *Shelby American World Registry*, Hertz revisited its GT350 rental program in 1969, and A. O. Smith produced 150 of the SportsRoof cars for them. These came on top of another 935 GT350 SportsRoof models and 1,536 GT500 SportsRoof cars. Convertible production broke down similarly, with 194 GT350s and 335 GT500 open cars

Automatic transmissions, a $30.54 option, outsold manual transmissions in the 1969 GT350 and 500. In Carroll Shelby's personal GT500, he preferred to shift gears for himself.

Under the large air cleaner lurked a single Holley four-barrel carburetor atop a mid-rise intake manifold. The GT500 package included a high-capacity fuel pump, die-cast aluminum valve covers, and a low-back-pressure dual-exhaust system.

leaving the Ionia shops. The total of cars produced in the United States came to 3,153. That distinction is significant, because, starting in 1967, Shelby had established a partnership with Mexican businessman Eduardo Velásquez.

Velásquez began his love affair with Shelby's Mustangs when, it appears, he purchased one of the Ken Miles/Phil Remington development notchback prototypes in 1965. He raced the car with a full-competition 289 engine and won in 10 out of 17 starts in three years. By 1966, Velásquez was Shelby's parts distributor for Mexico, and a year later, operating with Carroll as Shelby de México, S.A., they began modifying production coupes that they distributed through Mexican Ford dealerships from their own plant in Nuevo León. According to Velásquez, Ford Motor Company, S.A., the subsidiary in Mexico City, could produce only notchback coupes because import

regulations prohibited fastback and convertible models. Cars in 1967 and 1968 ran the 289, while their 1969 versions used 302s under their fiberglass hoods. The Shelby de México models got fiberglass trunk lids as well. Those cars manufactured in 1967 and 1968 retained their stock Mustang notchback lines, but for 1969 Velásquez and Shelby created a faux-fastback appearance by extending the rear side pillars (similar to several successful European racing cars) nearly to the end of the car body by using a fiberglass frame that they covered with black vinyl. Shelby de México produced 169 cars in 1967 and 203 in 1968. The 1969 model shown here is one of 306 production models that Velásquez offered in Emerald Green, Acapulco Blue, gold, black, white, and red. Shelby de México, S.A., suspended Mustang production in 1970 with the exception of one notchback race car. But the company resumed again

in 1971 with the Shelby GT351, of which they produced about 200.

Back home in California, while the disastrous 1968 Trans-Am season had slogged to its excruciating resolution, Ford had sent Shelby Racing a few new engines to test. It had redesigned portions of the ill-fated, oil-deprived 302 "tunnel-port" that had served Shelby so poorly. Engineering also sent a new 302 using the 351 Cleveland (Ford's other engine assembly plant) engine heads with canted valves that would go into the Boss series, and it offered him the Gurney-Eagle 302. A week after the championship season ended up in Kent, Washington, Shelby and team driver Horst Kwech were back out at Riverside testing for five days. The tunnel-port 302 proved to be the slowest. The Gurney-Eagle version ran the quickest. Fitting Weber carburetors to the canted-valve Boss engine made it 0.001 second faster than the intricate Gurney-Eagle engine.

For reasons of certification and assembly space, Ford could not start Boss 302 engine assembly until April 1969, which was too late for homologation. A thousand identical cars had to be completed for the car to race in the Trans-Am, and Shelby feared the risks of warranty claims on Gurney heads. Carroll, Kwech, and Phil Remington continued testing variations of tunnel-port engines and Boss 302s in 1968 and 1969 model cars. The Boss engine repeatedly proved better, stronger, faster, and

Dan Gurney (2) had his only drive in a Shelby-entered Boss 302 Mustang at Laguna Seca in 1969. Here, Gurney accelerates out of Turn 9 ahead of an older privateer Mustang. *David Friedman collection*

more reliable. In addition, Ford's chief engine engineer, Bill Gay, promised an adequate supply of the Cleveland heads at a reasonable price. In January, according to Vincent Liska in the *Shelby American Registry*, Ford's Dearborn assembly plant manufactured seven Mustang SportsRoof cars, each in white, without insulation or body sealer. The cars drove off the line with a 351W engine and four-speed transmissions, and went in three separate directions. One went to KarKraft, Ford's unofficial official race shop founded and operated by Roy Lunn

With 440 foot-pounds of torque, the driver of a 1969 GT500 might have felt like he could pull a train. Fastback GT350s and 500s started life as Mach 1s before the transformation at Shelby Automotive's Ionia, Michigan, plant.

Above: Eduardo Velázquez, a Shelby parts dealer in Mexico, created modified Mustangs starting in 1967. For the 1969 model year, he used coupes with vinyl-covered fiberglass C-pillar extensions to create a unique roofline. Production for '69 was 306 units.

Opposite page: All 1969 Shelby de México's cars used a 302-cubic-inch V-8. Mexican regulations required that at least 45 percent of the parts be made in Mexico. Rear axles, seat upholstery, and tires were some of the components made south of the border.

of the GT40 program after Henry Ford II ended that project in late 1967. Three went to Shelby, and the last three went to Bud Moore in South Carolina. (The KarKraft-prepared car ultimately went to Smokey Yunick, according to historian Dennis Begley, as a gift from Bunkie Knudsen for all of Yunick's successes during Knudsen's years at GM. The car never raced.)

Over the next six weeks, Shelby Racing pared 350 pounds from the cars and reconstructed them more to their liking. Trans-Am rules had relaxed somewhat, and suspensions and pieces now could come from aftermarket suppliers or other divisions of the parent company. Shelby found Lincoln Continental disc brakes and resurrected the 1965 GT350 over-ride traction bars. Engines, as delivered and tested from Ford, developed 470 horsepower.

Peter Revson joined Horst Kwech as team driver, and while the engines never let Shelby or Bud Moore down, it was one of those seasons that experienced drivers, owners, and journalists describe as "just racing." Mustangs finished second to Chevrolet, and Shelby's effort finished behind Bud Moore.

On December 10, 1969, Ford Public Affairs released an announcement from the chairman's office. Henry Ford II stated that Ford Motor Company would reduce its auto racing budget by 75 percent for 1970. "We think that we spent too much in 1969," Ford responded when someone asked him why. That left resources for only one Trans-Am effort for 1970, originating in South Carolina.

In an industry like automobile manufacturing, where powerful individuals have discretion in distributing enormous sums of money, loyalty and friendship are crucial ingredients in keeping a business relationship thriving. This explains Bunkie Knudsen's gift of a competition-ready Trans-Am car to former comrade-in-arms Smokey Yunick. However, while Bunkie Knudsen's arrival at Ford in February 1968 signaled support for Shelby's products, neither man knew the other. Henry Ford II had passed over 43-year-old Lee Iacocca, and so Iacocca wisely hunkered down and allowed whatever passing fancy had brought Knudsen to Ford Motor Company to run its course. The next man in line, however, looked at the calendar, and at age 45, Don Frey was 18 months older than Iacocca. He recognized that a clock was ticking, and Knudsen's arrival meant his chance to get the job had been postponed not only indefinitely but perhaps permanently.

On August 11, Frey submitted his resignation to Ford Motor Company. A month before that, Arjay Miller, another man whose career went astray with Knudsen's arrival, departed for Menlo Park, California, to head up Stanford University's School of Business. Since 1965, Frey had been Ford Division's general manager and its head product planner. Ford Motor Company's strength had been in his vision and imagination, and now his reward was far beyond the horizon. Since late 1961, he had been Carroll Shelby's champion at Ford's world headquarters.

Decades later, Frey explained things to Dave Friedman in *Remembering the Shelby Years*: "We kind of drifted back into racing. People like Carroll and Holman Moody would come by and we'd slip them a little something. There was no major summit meeting regarding our return to racing." Later Frey joked that, "whenever I walked out of [Shelby's] office, I always felt my pockets to make sure everything was there.

Shelby was using a more mainstream approach to pitching his road cars by 1968. No longer were competition results touted; now the emphasis was on the Grand Touring experience.

Even with the introduction of the potent 428 Cobra Jet engine in 1968, Shelby was advertising the GT500KR's standard safety and luxury features. Yet the new engine's accomplishments weren't ignored, as the Winternational results were used.

Top right: **As Shelby road cars gained weight in 1969, Shelby advertising highlighted the performance features of the GT350 and 500, acknowledging that the vehicles were GT automobiles with a touch of racing blood.**

Bottom right: **Shelby advertisements in 1966 stressed the competition heritage of the Cobra, going so far as highlighting significant race victories. The ads encouraged a brash, take-no-prisoners attitude.**

Convertible 1969 Shelby GT350s and 500s started life as base Mustangs with data code 76B Deluxe interior. A finished GT500 ragtop was priced at $5,027.

"The Cobra program turned out to be an incredible bargain for Ford. It all started on a shoestring, and much of it got buried in a '000' file somewhere, but that was no big deal. We all became spokesmen for that program and the rest is history." With Frey's departure, that line of history unraveled and broke. Those involved stepped and slipped elsewhere to new loyalties and new jobs. The outsiders drifted further outside.

From the outside, Ford again won Le Mans in 1969. John Wyer's *Gulf Mirages* came across the finish line on Sunday, June 15, in first and third place. Winners Jacky Ickx and Jackie Oliver drove 4,998 kilometers (3,123.4 miles), averaging 208.3 kilometers per hour (130.2 miles

per hour). Porsches and French-built Matra-Simca sport racers separated Fords from the nearest Ferrari, which was a North American Racing Team entry in eighth place, 574 kilometers (359 miles) behind the winners. Farther back in the field, Porsche tested the waters with three new 5-liter cars, the 917 long-tails. Like many first-year entries, they did not finish. That would not be the case in 1970.

The more Shelby's Mustangs evolved, the less charitably enthusiast magazines treated the man. Editors failed to recognize or refused to accept that nearly every decision

Above: **Nobody could ever say a Shelby road car didn't have presence, and the 1969 GT500 continued the tradition. It was a vehicle that was built for chasing the sun.**

Left inset: **Pulling next to this badge at a stoplight in 1969 was reason enough to look for a drag race somewhere else. The big-block Cobra Jet could propel the GT500 the length of the drag strip in 14 seconds at 102 miles per hour. Top speed was 115 miles per hour.** *Right Inset:* **The center-mounted cast-aluminum exhaust tip emitted a healthy rumble at idle, while revving the engine produced a head-turning snarl.**

Above: Long and lithe, the 1969 GT500 convertible was ideal for absorbing the passing environment. With the hefty 428 Cobra Jet engine under the hood, this Shelby road car was happiest on long stretches of straight tarmac.

Inset: Because the Cobra emblem was mounted on the C-pillar of 1969 Shelby road cars, the convertible models used the rear fender for the emblem.

Aerodynamics definitely played second fiddle to styling in the design of the 1969 Shelby road cars. The non-aero grille contributed to marginal fuel economy; on average, a driver could expect about 12 miles per gallon. But it sure looked great.

The fiberglass hood on the 1969 Shelby road cars was a piece of art. From behind the wheel, the hood seemed to go on forever.

the writer disliked came from code-named committees and unidentified department managers thousands of miles from California and perhaps light-years away from Shelby's philosophy—but only a phone call from Ford World Headquarters.

Car and Driver magazine's Brock Yates wrote eloquently. Yates was a man with vast experience and access to enough insider information to understand just what Ford Motor Company was doing with the Shelby-badged cars. Yates was cut from the same cloth as Carroll; he was a bit rebellious as Shelby was. Brock had organized

an already-legendary cross-country race, the Buck Baker Sea-to-Shining-Sea Memorial Dash—better known as the Cannonball Run—and his strong love of high-performance automobiles led him to occasional sadness and cynicism. He exorcised his frustration in print with a finely tuned typewriter. His text flowed in tidy contrast to dramatic and eye-catching photos of a new GT350 convertible.

"And so we come to the 1969 edition of the Shelby GT 350;" Yates wrote, "a garter snake in Cobra skin, affixed with dozens of name plates reading 'Shelby', 'Shelby-American', 'Cobra', and 'GT350' as if to constantly re-assure the owner that he is driving the real thing and not a neatly decorated Mustang (which he is)."

Alongside a dramatic photo looking across a vast field of hood interrupted by gentle rises, NACA slots, and NASCAR-style rotating hood-lock pins, the caption skewered the car: "The original Shelby GT350 was a fire-breather, it would accelerate, brake, and corner with a nimbleness only a Corvette could match. The GT350, 1969-style, is little more than a tough-looking Mustang Grande, a Thunderbird for Hell's Angels. Certainly not the car of Carroll Shelby's dreams." Among certain audiences, there is little doubt the value of early GT350s jumped after Yates' piece.

In truth, the car had gone beyond Shelby's wildest dreams. He really did invent a brand-new clapped-out sports car. It was a homologation trick in order to go racing and bring glory to Henry Ford II, Lee Iacocca, the Mustang, and the Blue Oval. The legacy that had led to the 1969 Shelby's appearance was huge. But the legacy drew in others, people of significance and influence who had their own style and taste.

Ford President Bunkie Knudsen was so taken with the '69 car's appearance that he went to Gene Bordinat and ordered him to integrate "the Shelby look" into Ford's styling for the 1971 Mustang. Even as magazine writers lambasted the look, Bordinat's advanced designers, insiders deep inside who survived with adaptable loyalties, stretched out new sheets of vellum and went back to work.

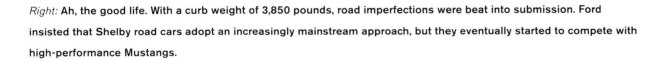

Right: Ah, the good life. With a curb weight of 3,850 pounds, road imperfections were beat into submission. Ford insisted that Shelby road cars adopt an increasingly mainstream approach, but they eventually started to compete with high-performance Mustangs.

Left inset: The steering wheel on the 1969 Shelby road cars was standard Mustang, including the rim-blow horn feature, except for the Shelby badge in the center. *Right inset:* For 1969, automatic transmissions outsold manuals, and Shelby road cars used wooden T-handles to select gears in the three-speed autoboxes.

CHAPTER SEVEN

THE ERA ENDS: 1970

Left: The only external difference between the 1969 and the 1970 GT350s were the black stripes on the hood and the installation of a Boss 302–sourced chin spoiler.

Below: Twin hood stripes recalled the early days of Shelby road cars, while differentiating the 1970 models from the prior year's offerings.

FOR SOME TIME NOW, BORDINAT'S DESIGNERS HAD BEEN FRANTICALLY ADAPTING WORKING DRAWINGS FROM FRONTS OF 1969 SHELBY-BASED PROTOTYPES TO MOLD ONTO THE 1971 KNUDSEN MUSTANG. On Wednesday, September 3, 1969, Ford introduced its 1970 models, including the carryover Shelby GT350s and GT500s. Then eight days later on Thursday, September 11, Henry Ford II fired Knudsen. It had been a whirlwind 583 days for the chairman, the president, and the company. Sadly, too deeply occupied with other things, Henry Ford II didn't think to send word to Bordinat and dismiss Knudsen's legacy of design as well. Knudsen's forceful personality and his strong ideas collided with Gene Bordinat and resulted in the next series of Mustangs that resembled Shelbys and, regrettably, Thunderbirds, whose noses looked like those from Pontiac Trans-Ams.

Some people closer to Henry Ford II, claimed it had been a maelstrom. As Knudsen roared down hallways always in a hurry to get things done, he stepped on too many toes and collided with too many egos as he shoved doors open too hard and moved on too fast. Others closer to the maelstrom said he simply pushed open Henry Ford II's door without knocking, signifying an assumption of equality that was never there and never could be there.

Above: A power-operated convertible top allowed the 1970 GT350 to be a multiple-season vehicle. The muffler was a transverse-mounted component.

Opposite page: Side stripes were offered in four colors: white, blue, black, and gold. The color of stripe depended on which of the dozen body hues a buyer chose.

A hint of blue from the air-cleaner assembly is visible through one of the exhaust vents on the hood of a 1970 Shelby GT350.

Shelby used the same cast-aluminum exhaust-system tip under the center of the 1970 GT350 and 500 rear bumper as he had in 1969. Back-up lights were stock Mustang units.

One of those individuals whom Knudsen rolled over and who had considered leaving was a man of equally strong personality and clever ideas.

"Iacocca was a hell of a politician," Shelby explained. "He had [Ford Finance director Ed] Lundy, he had [retired Ford Division general sales manager and his mentor] Charlie Beacham, whom Henry loved. He had so many friends on the board that Bunkie couldn't get anything done." But Iacocca also had grown more mature, learning from McNamara and working for the Deuce, as insiders called Henry Ford II. Lee Iacocca had badly wanted the job that went to the GM executive. Fiercely loyal to Henry Ford II, Iacocca rode out the 583 days of Knudsen while he remained executive vice president of North American Automobile Operations. After the dust from Knudsen's departure settled, to the chairman's relief and the company's good fortune, Lee Iacocca remained at Ford.

It was to Iacocca that Carroll Shelby turned in the middle of 1969. Shelby, another man of strong personality and smart ideas, had seen battles closing in around him. The cars that bore his name sold more copies as convertibles with air-conditioning and automatic transmissions than as unadorned performance coupes. Even the competitors, Camaro, Trans-Am, Barracuda, and Challenger, now sold less muscle and more luxury across the line. Perceptively, Shelby knew that cars with his name on them now competed against Ford Division's own Mach I and Boss 302 and 429 models. Shelby knew there were individuals within the corporation who resented that fact, and some had tried to diminish his influence and discount his success. There were those who diligently filed every form, dotted every "i" and crossed every "t," and then sat through countless meetings and watched their projects get bent, folded, spindled, and mutilated. Yet this outsider came in, shared jokes and drinks and with a nudge, a wink, and a handshake, had a new project, or as rumor

The Kamm-styled rear-end treatment tended to hold gasoline vapors close to the car's body. Until a recall in late 1969, backfires could, and did, ignite the vapors, scorching the bodywork.

had it, an entire model line, approved from on high, by 1973. But those who knew how to produce perfect papers also had learned how to undermine their enemies untraceably. They buried other Mustang high-performance development costs in his budgets. Shelby paid for much of the work on Knudsen's Boss 302 and 429 models without knowing it.

Outside the car enthusiast world, voices of public welfare and strident safety activists such as Ralph Nader began confronting automakers and challenging the need for 400-horsepower cars. Insurance companies countered the risk by simply raising premiums to be equal or exceed their high-risk (or "assigned-risk") policy-holders' monthly car payments. Even the critical affronts from longtime friends such as Brock Yates had begun to ache.

In the late summer of 1969, Shelby knew that the car and its sales were nothing like the old days. In July, A. O. Smith reported that it had 789 unsold 1969 models.

The frenzy had passed. Carroll knew that Mustangs were getting a new body and interior for 1971. Shelby went to Iacocca and Ford vice president and division general manager John Naughton.

"I told them it was never going to amount to anything more," Carroll recalled. "If you're going to build the cars, you have to have a racing program. It doesn't have to be a big program but you need to have a car that's out there because there's nothing that this car will do that's outstanding in performance, even with the 428." He asked them to end the Shelby Mustang program at the end of the 1970 model year. With little discussion, they agreed. In fact, this decision meant that all of the 1970 Shelbys would be leftover 1969 models, modified slightly and given new VIN tags.

To make the 1969 models attractive to Ford dealers who sold *new* cars, Shelby, A. O. Smith, and Ford Styling came up with a few cosmetic changes to make the cars

An owner-installed Hurst shifter handle in a 1970
GT350 was a performance touch that hearkened
back to earlier days.

Ambient air was fed to the air-cleaner
assembly of the 1970 GT350 from the
NACA duct in the center of the fiberglass
hood. While 1970 Mustangs used the
351 Cleveland small block, the Shelbys,
being built in 1969, were equipped with
the Windsor engine.

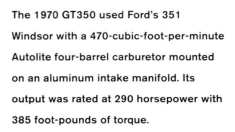

The 1970 GT350 used Ford's 351
Windsor with a 470-cubic-foot-per-minute
Autolite four-barrel carburetor mounted
on an aluminum intake manifold. Its
output was rated at 290 horsepower with
385 foot-pounds of torque.

All 1970 Shelbys were leftover 1969 models, modified slightly and given new VIN tags under supervision of the Federal

Bureau of Investigation. Only 194 GT350 convertibles were built for the 1969/1970 model years.

High-back seats were lifted directly from the Mustang. By 1970, most Shelby modifications were largely cosmetic.

A 140-mile-per-hour speedometer was a touch optimistic—a 1970 GT350 might see 115 miles per hour flat-out. But it's a Shelby, and it needed the big numbers.

look different from the 1969s. That was the easy part. The legal part required the cooperation of the Federal Bureau of Investigation.

For an automobile to be titled as a 1969 or 1970 model, the vehicle identification number, the VIN, changes slightly. As Vincent Liska pointed out in the *Shelby American World Registry,* VIN numbers for cars manufactured in 1969 began with a 9, while those assembled in 1970 began with a 0. Shelby and A. O. Smith notified the FBI, which handles interstate jurisdiction, and they sent

agents to oversee the process of making old cars new.

Ford had mounted identification numbers at the base of the windshield, on the inner fenders, and on door data plates. A. O. Smith personnel, under the watchful eye of FBI agents, removed each windshield and VIN plate, mounted a new plate and replaced the windshield. They also replaced the stickers on the doors. The federal agents kept track of vehicles, collected the 1969-issue plates, and supervised their destruction. When Smith personnel explained the unlikelihood of anyone dismantling a car

A screen prevented debris from being sucked into the functional side scoop on 1970 Shelby convertibles.

Only one wheel design was offered in 1970, a design using a cast-aluminum center and chromed 15x7-inch steel rim. An 11.3-inch front disc-brake rotor filled the wheel.

to find the third plate on the inner fender wall, FBI agents pointed out that U.S. law required VIN numbers in only two locations.

Hoods on the 1970 models lost the two rear heat-extractor NACA ducts and stylists added wide flat black panels extending from the two lower hood ducts. A. O. Smith assemblers packed front chin-spoilers, similar to Boss 302s, in the trunk of each GT350 and GT500. Cars would not fit on transporters with the spoilers glued in place.

Throughout 1970, A. O. Smith renumbered a total of only 789 GT350s and GT500s, roughly one-fourth of the two-year production run of 3,153 similar cars. This was not even a measurable fraction of the record sales numbers that Ford Division had achieved in the first year of the Mustang. But then again, Shelby sales were never meant to do that.

In Trans-Am racing for 1970, Ford reclaimed its title against an exceptionally aggressive field of Camaros, AMX cars, Dodge Challengers, Plymouth Barracudas, and Pontiac Firebirds. Bud Moore started the season with Parnelli Jones

Entry into the back seats required a bit of flexibility, but the surroundings were worth the effort. The roll bar was bolted in, rather than welded, as was the norm until 1968.

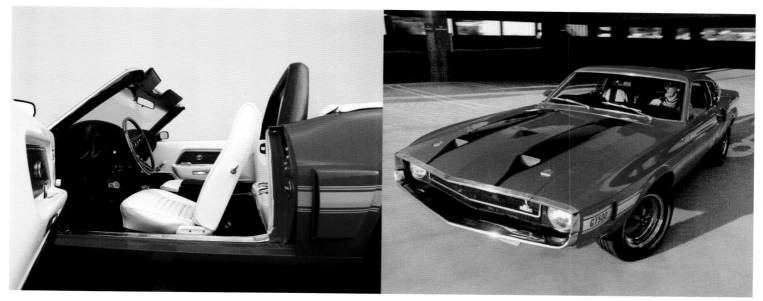

The center console in the 1970 GT350 was sourced from the Mercury Cougar. Carroll Shelby was less than pleased with the direction his automobiles were headed—away from performance. But Ford was calling the shots at this stage.

The 4-inch extension to the front of the 1970 Shelby GT500 is apparent from this perspective. With a rear window of this size, air conditioning was more a necessity than a luxury.

in a single car. When the final checkered flag fell, Parnelli won 5 out of 11 races and beat Mark Donohue in Roger Penske's AMX team by a single point. Ford took third place with the addition of George Follmer, who accomplished eight podium finishes including one first and five second places behind his teammate. In 1970, Carroll Shelby was nowhere to be found.

He wasn't alone in isolation or exclusion. At Le Mans, Porsche got it right with its 917s, which took first and second. Not a single entrant tried his luck with Ford's GT40s. John Wyer and Grady Davis switched loyalties as

well to Porsche, although their three 917s did not finish. (A year later, in 1971, a John Wyer/Gulf Oil 917 would take second at the 24-hour race.) And then they were gone, too.

Like other limited-production automobiles, the Shelby Mustangs were always intended to be cars produced for a limited audience with clear and particular tastes. Up through their final evolution in 1970, these "personal" cars still fit precisely into the Iacocca Fairlane Committee concept of the Mustang as Total Performance—Powered by Ford. In recognition of that achievement, Ford Motor Company named Iacocca president on December 10, 1970.

It's said that the mark of a good designer is knowing when to lift the pen, and the 1970 GT500 is evidence of that. Timeless proportions never go out of style.

The 4-inch extension to the front of the 1970 Shelby GT500 is apparent from this perspective.

A 1970 GT500 was made to move, and with the 428 Cobra Jet engine under the long hood, it could step out with authority. A 0–60 mile-per-hour time of 6.0 seconds was admirable, especially for a 3,850-pound vehicle.

The 428 Cobra Jet engine was a tight squeeze in the 1970 GT500. Such cramped confines led Ford to insist that any size engine in the lineup fit the 1971 Mustang with ease.

Deeply tunneled instruments were straight from the Mach 1. Almost all of Shelby Automotive's modifications in 1970 involved exterior body parts, not extensive interior changes.

CHAPTER EIGHT

THE LEGEND RETURNS:
2000 AND BEYOND

Left: Circular fog lamps hearken to the Cobra models of the 1990s, while the aggressive grille is reminiscent of the 1968 GT500KR. Ford's stylists did a masterful job integrating former Shelby cues.

Below: With the Camaro and Firebird swept from the scene, the GT500 will directly threaten the Chevrolet Corvette, for thousands less. Ford is starting the pricing at $39,999.

Bold, striking, and expensive, the GT500E with an optional 525-horsepower engine starts at $189,000. With that much power, driving school is a must.

WORD SPREAD FAST. There was a new Jerry Bruckheimer movie coming. He was remaking the 1974 car-cult classic *Gone in 60 Seconds*. The original film starred a 1973 Ford Mustang Mach I. There were actors in it, too, but few people remember their names. Now Bruckheimer had Oscar winners and nominees Nick Cage, Angelina Jolie, and Robert Duvall. And, more importantly, he had a customized 1967 Shelby GT500.

As the script moved through development, production manager Jeff Mann called on hot-rod designer and illustrator Steve Sanford to develop a character car for the climactic chase scenes. Nicolas Cage, playing Randall "Memphis" Raines, had retired from a successful career

stealing cars in Los Angeles, only to be called back into service when his younger brother Kip bungled a contract to provide 50 cars in five days to a particularly nasty client. These weren't just any cars, however, but a very specific list, ranging from a 1999 Aston Martin DB7 to a 1957 Chevrolet Bel Air convertible, to a Humvee pickup, to the Shelby GT500. To keep the inventory straight, to throw off eavesdropping, wiretapping police, and probably to appeal better to the male audience, each car got a woman's name. The Aston was Mary, the Chevy was Stefanie, the Humvee became Tracy

Above: **Looking like a still from** *Gone in 60 Seconds,* **the GT500E continuation cars are modified fastbacks that Unique Performance massages into Eleanor clones.**

Top left inset: **Order the standard 302-cubic-inch engine in the GT500E and 325 horsepower are on tap. Optional engines raise the output up to 725 horsepower.** *Top right inset:* **Like Shelby road cars from the 1960s, sequential turn signals span the rear end. A badge covers the area where the fuel filler originally went.**

and the Shelby was, naturally, Eleanor. She would be the last car stolen, Cage's treasure, and the car to provide the film with its wildest chases and jumps. It was, in short, the perfect role for a Shelby GT500.

From Stanford's designs, Mann involved Chip Foose to fabricate a prototype body in wood and clay. Then Mann went to Ray Claridge and his company, Cinema Vehicles in North Hollywood. Claridge is the oldest and biggest picture-car fabricator in the business. Because the Eleanor

of the first film had suffered a disastrous fate, Bruckheimer and Mann anticipated that bad things would befall this Eleanor as well. So Claridge built 12 picture cars using 1967 fastbacks that he found and converted. They built a reinforced coil-over front suspension with rack-and-pinion steering. Engines ranged from a tired 289 to a blueprinted 400-horsepower Ford "351 crate motor." Eleven of the cars saw film time, but they made stunt drivers crazy, because Claridge built each one for a separate duty, sideways slides,

Left: Unique Performance makes a pair of very-high-performance road cars, both with the blessing of Carroll Shelby: The GT350SR and the GT500E. Just bring lots of money.

Above: Faired-in side scoops direct cooling air to the massive rear brakes, while Torq-Thrust wheels lend a period flavor.

Above: **The GT350SR maintains the use of the rocker stripe that Pete Brock started with the 1965 GT350.**

Opposite page left: **It's like buying a brand-new clapped-out race car, again. Except this is meant for street use—fast street use.**

Opposite page right: **The use of a 1965 GT350R front apron directs cooling air into the radiator, a good thing when the base 331-cubic-inch engine develops 410 horsepower.**

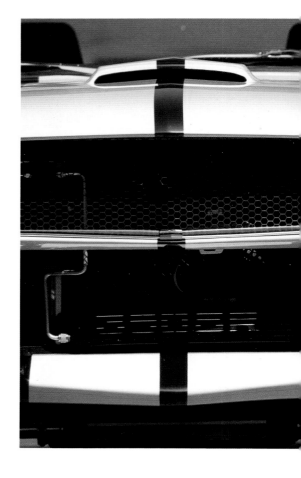

spins, high-speed sprints, or jumps, so each one drove differently. The twelfth was there as well, sliced down the middle lengthwise for interior scenes, where large cameras would not fit inside a normal automobile. Students of the film already know that only seven of the cars survived to join Claridge's rental stock.

By the time filming ended, Cinema Vehicles had completed a thirteenth Eleanor, built on an actual 1967 GT500 body. It went into Jerry Bruckheimer's garage, a perk that producers can provide for themselves.

The frenzy that Eleanor caused spilled over onto dozens of aftermarket parts makers and eventually it launched a project known as the Shelby Continuations, from a company in Texas called Unique Performance. Their first car, the Shelby GT500E with several engine options, appeared in early 2003 and it strongly resembled

the Stanford/Foose/Claridge Eleanor car. Douglas Hasty, Unique's president, introduced a second model, the GT350SR, in November 2003. His staff fitted the car with a 331-cubic-inch Ford engine developing 410 horsepower and four-wheel disc brakes. They set a base price of $109,000 for it or the GT500E. In late March 2005, the company announced its big-block fuel-injected GT500E convertible with a 427-cubic-inch V-8 that, depending on options selected, developed between 525 and 725 horsepower. Prices for the 525 horsepower version start at $189,000. Unique Performance takes original 1965 through 1968 Mustangs and converts them into their own products.

Through the 1990s and early 2000s, Ford's Special Vehicles Team, SVT, had performed its own modifications to Mustangs. At the New York Auto Show in March 2005, Ford, SVT, and Carroll Shelby announced their newest

collaboration, the Shelby Cobra GT500, which Ford will offer in mid-2006 as a 2007 model. After years of separation, not always pleasant for either side, Ford and Shelby reunited to work on the Ford GT, a project inspired by the GT40s that Shelby took to victory at Le Mans for Henry Ford II. That led to the next logical step: the new Mustang.

"John Coletti brought me back there," Carroll explained. "And Billy Ford invited me in and said, 'We'd like you to finish things out with us if it's okay with you?' I told him I'd love it. We never argued over a thing. They're setting up the production line now on what they call the Shelby Mustang. They did everything right."

Recalling 1969 nomenclature, the Cobra GT500 will use Ford's 5.4-liter "modular" V-8 for power. This is part of an engine family that's been in production for more than a decade. Ford engineering introduced it with a 4.6-liter

version. This configuration is supercharged, and with dual-overhead cams and four valves per cylinder, it develops 450 horsepower and 450 foot-pounds of torque. The engine adopts the aluminum cylinder heads, piston rings, and bearings, as well as forged pistons and connecting rods from the modular engine in Ford's GT. Ford introduced this variation in milder tune in the 2000 SVT Mustang Cobra R with a limited run of just 300 cars. Ford couples this to its T-56 six-speed manual transmission that has proven itself with the Cobra R and in the FR500C Racing Mustangs in the Grand-Am series.

"When you consider the pony cars of the 1960s," Ford SVT program engineer Tom Jones explained in Ford preview materials, "today's engines produce approximately double the horsepower, four times the fuel economy, and 100 times fewer emissions." Ford's modular V-8 family of

Above: With 450-plus horsepower, the 2007 GT500 is a tire dealer's dream come true. Its SVT development ensures that it will be durable and fast—very fast.

Left: The large rear wing contributes downforce on the rear tires, an advantage when an automobile has as much speed potential as the 2007 GT500.

Left inset: The heart of any Shelby or SVT product is the engine, and the 2007 GT500 does not come up short. Its 5.4-liter engine uses a screw-type supercharger and an air-to-water intercooler to generate in excess of 450 horsepower and 450 foot-pounds of torque.

Center inset: Like the Mustang GT that was the starting point for the GT500 project, the large badge on the rear panel is for decoration only. The actual fuel-filler door is located on the driver's side of the car.

Right inset: Mustang senior designer Keith Rogman used the GT-R concept as the basis for the fascia, including the imposing grille opening.

engines develops more horsepower than anything out of any Ford assembly plant in the past, yet highway fuel economy that peaked at 11 miles per gallon with a judiciously driven (and rarely accelerated) GT500KR, exceeds 20 miles per gallon on the highway in the Mod V-8, while meeting U.S. government Low Emissions Vehicle LEV-II tailpipe emissions standards.

"People may not realize that typical 'hot-rodding' techniques involve improving an engine's efficiency to extract more power from every ounce of fuel that is burned," said SVT chief vehicle engineer Jay O'Connell. "It's an unexpected benefit that automakers get from racing—the tricks to winning on the racetrack can help make cleaner, more fuel-efficient vehicles for the street.

"We apply our Ford GT engine experience to the GT500 to bring over 450 horsepower to a much bigger enthusiast audience," O'Connell continued. "It really delivers on the essence of two great names in Ford performance—a mix of SVT's modern-day experience with supercharging and the Shelby GT500's heritage of big-block power."

The new GT500 uses a MacPherson strut front suspension incorporating reverse-L lower control arms and a 34-mm 1.33-inch tubular anti-sway bar. To create an even-quicker steering response on the already rigid chassis, SVT's engineers added shock-tower bracing and a "K" structural member, much like the early Shelby Export Braces and Monte Carlo Bars. At the rear, SVT has configured the three-link solid-rear-axle system based on the FR500C racers. This incorporates constant-rate coil springs, a tubular Panhard rod for precise axle location control, and a 24-mm 0.94-inch solid rear sway bar. Rear shocks sit outside the rear structural rails, near the wheels, to decrease the lever effect of the axle while allowing a

more precise and slightly softer tune in the shock valving. The 2005 coupe is already 31 percent stiffer in torsional rigidity than the 2004 models. The car sits an inch lower than standard Mustang GT models. Brembo 14-inch-diameter discs up front and 13-inch rear discs provide stopping power to match the engine's speed potential. Ford specifies P255/45R19 tires on 19x9.5 machined-aluminum wheels all around to meet acceleration, handling, and braking needs.

"Coletti had it all done for this car," Carroll explained. "By the time Ford would have gotten it into production, it was five million dollars. So Phil Martens decided that they would do away with it. Well, it turns out that I agree with that decision.

"It costs you two hundred pounds of additional weight. The cars that they put it on, the two or three development prototypes, weren't any faster around the tight handling circuit or their big track. And the way Hau Thai-Tang's guys have worked on this thing and worked on it, to tell you the truth, I wouldn't spend the five million dollars either.

Critics have questioned why Ford, which had offered an independent rear suspension on its last SVT Cobra, did not bring that technology along to the new Mustang, and especially to the GT500. While an element of Shelby's solid-axle heritage was apparent, the real decision was simpler, like the results Ken Miles and Phil Remington achieved in hours whirling around Willow Spring Race Track in the Mojave Desert north of Los Angeles. It just wasn't necessary.

"We spent a lot of time at the track developing the new Mustang," Hau Thai-Tang explained in several interviews at the New York Auto Show introduction. Thai-

Tang served as chief engineer for the 2005 Mustang and soon after its introduction, Ford moved him to SVT. While drag racers prefer solid axles, he worked hard to develop a car that was not limited strictly to astonishing straight-line performance. Shelby Mustangs were road racers primarily, and that heritage played heavily in decisions about this new car. Thai-Tang's goal with the new Mustang was "ensuring it was capable of handling future performance derivatives," he explained. "In terms of performance, the Mustang's solid rear-axle setup in the GT500 has been proven in race competition this year with a Mustang FR500C taking the checkered flag at the season-opening Grand-Am Cup race at Daytona. First race, first win; not bad against the best from Germany and Japan." For the record, the Mustangs finished first, second, and ninth against BMW M3s, Porsche 996s, Cadillac CTS-VSs, and Nissan 350Zs.

A first in Shelby design are the covered headlights seen on the 2007 GT500 concept car. The aggressive, angular grille is reminiscent of years past.

Huge 14-inch vented and cross-drilled discs, squeezed by Brembo brakes, reside in the front 19x9.5-inch machined-aluminum wheels. The tires are P255/45R19s, but they can be overcome with the 5.4-liter's 450-plus horsepower.

SVT design director Doug Gafka had a wealth of visual heritage to draw upon for the new car, and he picked and chose judiciously. Peter Brock's stripes, on the hood, roof, and rear deck advance the tradition, as do the model-designation stripes along the rocker panel. "The GT500's wide grille openings are imposing," Gafka said, "like a drop-jawed Cobra ready to strike. If you saw that look coming in your rearview mirror, it would make you move out of the way quickly."

"The new Mustang has classic design cues from some of the best-looking Mustangs of all time, including the Shelbys," Keith Rogman explained. Rogman is Mustang senior designer. "The design of the GT500 has been at the forefront of our minds since the outset of the entire Mustang program. The more aggressive fascia is actually a race-car design," he continued, "borrowed from the

Mustang GT-R concept. It works well with the overall look of the GT500 because racing has such a strong connection with Shelby.

"We've taken leather design trends [for the interior] to a new level by using it on almost every exposed surface in the GT500," Rogman added. "Leather has long been a performance fashion accessory for enthusiasts, from jackets to racing gloves, so it perfectly matches all the other driving-oriented cues."

Reminiscent of Shelby's first GT350, Rogman and his colleagues completely wrapped the interior in black. However, he used the leather everywhere that Shelby had black paint or vinyl. Leather covers the dashboard, the door panels, and the center armrest, the shift lever, the boot, and parking-brake handle. SVT's signature red appears in seat and door panel inserts to provide a striking

If it was a plastic surface in the Mustang GT, it's been covered in leather in the 2007 GT500 concept car. Great ergonomics promise that the Shelby will be a comfortable cross-country vehicle.

contrast in small doses. On the instrument panel, titanium faces with white lettering stare back at the driver. SVT engineers repositioned instruments so the most prominent is the large tachometer on the right side of the main pairing, balanced with an equal-size speedometer on the left. At night, owners can modify the color of the illuminated letters and numbers with the MyColor color-configuration system to make some 125 unique color options. It is outside the

car, however, where the Shelby Cobra/Cobra Coupe/Shelby Mustang legacy shines through.

"The process we created," O'Connell continued, "while working on the body design of the Ford GT really helped us come up with the functional front air splitter and rear spoiler for the GT500. It was essential that they provide measurable downforce at high speeds without detracting from the classic design."

Far left: **At the other end of the shift knob is a T-56 six-speed manual transmission, which is connected to a 3.31:1 ratio rear axle.**

Left: **At the hub of the tri-spoke steering wheel is an air-bag cover that doesn't let you forget what you're piloting. Cruise-control buttons line the wheel's spokes for easy access.**

For 40 years, enthusiasts have cherished and craved that classic design. Countless body shops, speed merchants, and aftermarket suppliers have helped thousands of early Mustang owners pay homage to the legacy and character of Carroll Shelby's answer to Lee Iacocca's challenge.

For those who missed buying a Shelby Mustang the first time around, there are owners and restorers happy to part with their treasures now for fair prices—some 20 to 40 times the original cost—considering the pleasure and excitement buyers will get for their investment. For others, looking for an update on the timeless theme packed with bragging-rights horsepower as well as a certified link to Carroll Shelby himself, the continuation cars fill that demand. Whether they will achieve the cachet (or the return on investment) of the original cars is a fair question.

Now there are the new cars. Just after Ford introduced the new Mustang, Ford's vice president of product creation for North American operations, Phil Martens, promoted Hau Thai-Tang to the job of directing SVT's operations. Just after the Special Vehicles Team announced the Shelby Cobra GT500 in New York City, *Motor Trend* magazine's Todd Lassa spoke with the 38-year-old engineer. Lassa

learned that, like many of his colleagues, Thai-Tang has cars he admires. His choice is Porsche's 911.

"These [cars] have a timeless quality about them," Thai-Tang told Lassa by way of explanation. "There are evolutionary design changes. That sense of timelessness just fascinates me."

Ford Motor Company and Phil Martens could not possibly have selected a better individual, a better organization, and a better time to bring out the new Mustang and to bring back Carroll Shelby's GT500. Thai-Tang and Shelby have delivered to the public Ford's new version of timelessness, and it's a 450-horsepower romp down memory lane, complete with a full warranty, leather interior, six-speed transmission, four-wheel disc brakes, variable-color instrument panel, and a pile of quintessential CDs programmed in the changer. This is no "brand-new clapped-out race car." Instead, it's the vehicle to implant brand-new experiences alongside the longing to relive old memories, real and imagined. It should be fascinating just to watch Ford's and Shelby's evolutionary design changes that are still ahead.

INDEX